Success Is a Low-Probability Game

Success Is a Low-Probability Game

Anuj Jain and Anshika Jain

ink | OCCAM

ISBN: 978-93-6547-439-8

First published in India 2025
This edition published 2025

BluOne Ink Pvt. Ltd
A-76, 2nd Floor, Sector 136, Noida
Uttar Pradesh 201301
www.bluone.ink
publisher@bluone.ink

Printed and bound in India by Thomson Press (India) Ltd

Kali and Occam are imprints of BluOne Ink

ink | OCCAM

Contents

Authors' Note

We have made our best effort to make this book an engaging read. We would love to hear different perspectives from readers after reading this book. We are confident that those with more experience than us will have valuable insights to contribute to the next edition of this book. Happy reading!

Authors' Note

[illegible]

1

Define Your Goal: Understand What It Takes

'The first step in achieving your goal is to take a moment to respect your goal. Know what it MEANS to you to achieve it.'

—Dwayne Johnson

We have divided this discussion into the following parts:

- Understand your goal or destination before you start the journey.
- Why do you want to accomplish a particular goal? Be sure and have your own reasons for pursuing it.
- Never choose a goal just because others have chosen it.
- Be strategic; analyse the opportunity. Right place, right time.
- Understand the reward before committing to a goal.
- If your goal is to reach the peak of Mount Everest, identify intermediate destinations along the way.
- Conduct a gap assessment.

Understand Your Goal or Destination before You Start the Journey

In simpler terms, to reach your goal, you first need to know what it is!

The first step before starting your journey is to clearly understand and define your goal. For example, it could be cracking a competitive exam (such as civil services, an engineering entrance, or the chartered accountancy course), building a new-age business or startup, or representing your country in sports.

Goals should be Specific, Measurable, Achievable, Realistic, and Time-bound (SMART).

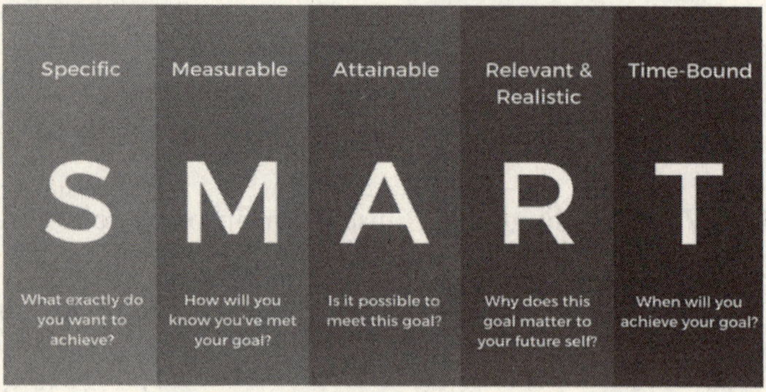

The concept of SMART goals.

Source: There's a SMART Way to Write Management's Goals and Objectives by George T. Doran

The goal-setting process outlined above provides a broad overview. This book explores all these aspects, along with the challenges involved, in detail across various sections.

Why Do You Want to Accomplish a Particular Goal?

When deciding to pursue a goal, an individual should undertake a holistic analysis of various factors. These include personal motivational drivers, the resources required and their availability, the reasons for choosing a particular goal, and the reasons for not selecting other alternatives.

It can also be beneficial for aspirants to assess all possible options—evaluating every potential goal that comes to mind—before determining the reasons for choosing a specific one.

Real-Life Example: Evaluating Different Opportunities with a Structured Approach

One day, we decided to build our own business. We sat down with a blank sheet of paper and considered all possible options, including:

- Becoming a seller on an e-commerce platform
- Building a tech-based platform or marketplace for specific goods or services
- Starting derivative trading
- Starting a cloud kitchen or restaurant

We then evaluated each option by considering various factors, such as:

- How much time could we realistically dedicate to the new business?
- Would we start and manage it alone, or would we need a co-founder?
- What knowledge or resources would be required beyond time and money?
- Did we have relevant experience or skills necessary for any of the options? For example:
  - Marketing skills for becoming a successful e-commerce seller

  - Coding/tech skills to build a prototype of a tech platform
  - Analytical skills and financial expertise for derivative trading
- What was our core strength, and where could we best leverage it?
- Would we need to quit our jobs to build the business, or could we work on it alongside our jobs initially?
- What were our long-term growth plans for each option?
- What were our motivational drivers for each choice?

After carefully evaluating all these factors, we decided to pursue derivative trading for the following reasons:

- Our educational background in finance, accounting, and taxation provides us with a solid understanding of financial instruments.
- We could easily grasp financial market concepts such as price action, trends, momentum, moving averages, and technical indicators.
- We could continue our jobs while using our savings as capital for the new business.
- We could start with passive trading strategies, such as positional strategies, which would not require us to be in front of a screen making frequent decisions—allowing for safer bets with reasonable returns.
- We did not require a co-founder, as Anshika could manage trade execution while we made strategic decisions together.
- In case of unfavourable outcomes, we would still have other income sources, including passive income from savings and salaries.

- We would continuously explore growth opportunities, such as starting our own trading desk or launching a fund, and assess what would be needed for such expansion.

We initially considered at least five to seven other options. We applied equal effort in evaluating each one and carefully identified the reasons for eliminating them. This exercise proved invaluable later when we faced challenges along the journey, helping us to stay focused and avoid confusion.

In summary, before an individual starts investing time and resources, there is still an opportunity to reconsider and change the chosen goal. However, once the goal is decided, one must adopt the 'all-in' approach, which is discussed in detail in Chapter 5.

Never Choose a Goal Just Because Others Have Chosen It

An aspirant's attributes and motivational drivers play a crucial role in determining both the process and the likelihood of achieving a goal. The probability of success varies for each individual, depending on their unique strengths and motivations. For example, if someone aims to crack a competitive exam, factors such as past academic performance, competence in foundational concepts, and problem-solving skills become critical.

If an aspirant lacks the necessary attributes for achieving a particular goal, their initial probability of success may be lower compared to others. However, such attributes cannot be developed overnight.

Overcoming these gaps requires continuous effort, exposure to challenges, and consistent hard work to drive meaningful improvement.

Consider the example of building a successful start-up. According to publicly available research reports, nearly 90 per cent of start-ups fail. Moreover, even a founder with a previously successful venture has only a 30 per cent chance of success in their next one.

If your primary motivation for launching a start-up is simply to add the coveted tag of 'founder' to your name, or if you are pursuing this path merely because your university peers are doing the same, you may soon find yourself in a difficult situation.

It is possible that others in your cohort have made their decision after carefully weighing all the key factors, while you are simply following a trend driven by peer pressure. However, success in the start-up world demands strong individual conviction, resilience, and strategic planning—qualities that cannot be substituted by external influences.

Remember, the people around you will change over the course of your journey, or even throughout your life, but your goal remains your own. Never choose a goal under external pressure.

A difficult truth to accept is that your friends today may become your competitors tomorrow. While collaboration is valuable, it is essential to ensure that your goal aligns with your personal strengths, motivations, and long-term aspirations rather than being a mere reaction to what others around you are doing.

Real-Life Example: Accomplishing Challenging Goals Would Require Determination for Turning Weaknesses into Strengths

After completion of my tenth-grade exams, I (Anuj) wanted to choose commerce with computer science for two reasons:

- I was good at computer science but struggled with mathematics.
- My crush had also opted for commerce with computer science, and I wanted to be in the same classroom as her.

However, my parents insisted that I take commerce with mathematics. I had no interest in mathematics and saw no purpose in learning concepts like straight lines, differentiation, integration, or trigonometry.

My parents took me to multiple counsellors who guided me through the career implications of choosing commerce with computer science versus commerce with mathematics. I eventually understood that commerce with mathematics was the more logical option, primarily because it would prepare me for future competitive exams. Thus, I decided to choose commerce with mathematics in class 11. This decision presented two major challenges:

- Staying away from my crush
- Finding meaning and interest in mathematical concepts like differentiation and trigonometry

In my first evaluation exams in class 11, I topped in accounting, business studies, and economics. However, my performance in mathematics was disastrous—I scored just 6 out of 100. The journey from scoring 6 marks to 90 marks was incredibly difficult. I worked hard for an entire year, and with my best friend's support, I gradually improved.

Looking back, choosing commerce with mathematics was one of the best decisions I ever made. It played a significant role in my journey to becoming a chartered accountant (CA) and company secretary (CS). To this day, my knowledge of mathematics has been invaluable in both my professional career and entrepreneurial journey.

The key takeaway from the above example is that it is possible to transform a weakness into a strength. However, this requires dedication, sacrifices, and consistent hard work to achieve the desired goal.

From a mathematical perspective, a challenging goal is one with a low probability of success. This means that if you choose a difficult path, many others pursuing the same goal may not reach the final destination. People will get eliminated at various stages of the journey for different reasons.

A crucial point to remember is that while you may start your journey alongside friends or peers, there is a possibility that you will have to continue alone at some stage—or even at the very end when you achieve your goal. For instance, consider the civil services examination. The process involves multiple stages: preliminary exam, mains exam, and the interview/personality test. Ultimately, only a small percentage of candidates successfully qualify and receive an offer to join the civil services. This illustrates that while many start the journey, only a select few reach the final destination.

Real-Life Example: Making Career Choices Based on Growth Potential, Not Comfort

When I (Anuj) completed my IPCC exam (CA Intermediate), the next step was to find an internship opportunity. My best friend and I attended multiple interviews at CA firms. I received a few offers, but unfortunately, my friend did not, as he had only cleared one of the two groups of the IPCC exam.

Despite this, we decided that we wanted to join a firm together—one that would offer both of us an internship position. Through some referrals, we managed to secure offers from a good CA firm and started our internship together.

However, I was not satisfied with the kind of exposure I was getting. My peers and seniors were not particularly driven, nor were they eager for learning and growth. On the other hand, my friend was content with the opportunity.

I found it difficult to adjust to the firm, and after a few months, I decided to explore better opportunities. One day, I received an offer from one of the top firms in town. After careful thought, I decided to quit my current firm for better career prospects.

The new firm had a stellar track record, an amazing learning environment, and tremendous growth opportunities. Meanwhile, my friend continued his internship at the previous firm for the entire tenure.

The exposure I gained in the new firm played a crucial role in helping me clear my CA Final exam on my first attempt, whereas my friend had to struggle through multiple attempts.

Moreover, after completing my CA exams, I secured a career opportunity in the exact field I wanted to pursue—transaction advisory. The only reason I was able to break into this field was my internship experience at the second firm. Had I not taken the difficult decision to switch firms, and had I continued with my friend out of comfort or sentiment, the eventual outcome might not have been as favourable for me.

Be Strategic; Analyse the Opportunity

When pursuing a goal that involves an undefined path—such as building a new-age business—it is crucial to analyse the opportunity carefully and position yourself at the right place and at the right time.

For example, the quick commerce boom in India presented a lucrative opportunity due to shifts in consumer behaviour and a large addressable market.

Entrepreneurs who entered at the right time, such as Blinkit, Zepto, and Instamart, were able to capitalize on this trend effectively.

However, if someone were to launch a similar quick commerce business today, it may not be a wise decision unless there is a significant value gap to address or a compelling new value proposition.

Established players, like those mentioned earlier, have already secured key advantages such as infrastructure, capital, and a loyal customer base, making it difficult for new entrants to disrupt the market without a strong differentiator.

Thus, when choosing a goal in an undefined path, the focus should be on identifying existing gap and capitalizing on a futuristic, game-changing opportunity that addresses those gaps effectively. Strategic foresight and timing can make all the difference in success or failure.

Understand the Reward before Committing to a Goal

When evaluating different challenging goals, a common question arises: 'Can I choose a goal that is highly rewarding?' The answer depends on the type of goal chosen.

Below are two categories of goals that often lead to significant rewards:

Revolutionary (or Innovative) Ideas

These are ideas with a low probability of success but a high potential impact on society. If successfully implemented, they can lead to massive financial rewards and societal transformation.

Let's take the example of new-age quick commerce companies. These companies have significantly changed consumer behaviour. Before they emerged, consumers used to buy groceries from nearby departmental stores. The idea of a company delivering grocery items to customers' doorsteps was unique. This concept had a large market and a significant impact.

Over the years, many operational challenges must have arisen during the implementation of this idea. However, these companies have captured a significant market share. There has been a shift from consumers visiting the nearest departmental store to ordering groceries at any time, with items being delivered to their doorsteps within ten minutes.

The consumers are still buying the same products—there has been no new product development. However, a revolutionary service has been introduced, influencing consumer behaviour and making home grocery delivery a key necessity.

There are multiple similar examples. Consider, for instance, a company that invented a COVID-19 vaccine. The entire world wanted this vaccine, and many people were willing to pay the highest possible price to obtain it.

The purpose of the above examples is to illustrate that if an aspirant seeks substantial rewards, an idea that has a significant impact on society may be a good choice. However, a detailed evaluation—including risk assessment and other factors discussed later in this book—is equally critical. Since these ideas are unconventional, their successful execution may not be straightforward. Ultimate success and the realization of rewards are not guaranteed. For a first mover, the probability of success is often low. Just think—if the probability of success were high, this idea might have already been implemented.

Ideas That Have a Strong Impact on a Small Fraction of Society

With changing lifestyles—reduced sleep, poor diet, and unhealthy consumption habits—and sometime due to heredity, a new problem has become apparent in males (especially in tier 1 cities)—male pattern baldness.

Over time, many solutions have emerged, ranging from medication to surgical procedures. Medications, including globally approved ones, have been successful in deferring the problem—evident in the reduction of hair fall for a few years. However, they have shown limited success in hair regrowth, merely postponing hair loss. Surgical solutions come with their own challenges, including post-surgical maintenance and variable outcomes.

Let's consider a specific target group of customers affected by male pattern baldness. For example, if an aspirant develops a proven solution to this problem, they will have the ability to charge a significant premium from certain customers. Many of these customers might even be willing to pay a success fee if the problem is fully resolved.

Similar patterns have been observed with various surgical solutions for different medical conditions—for instance, treatments for infertility.

The key takeaway is that an aspirant can identify a specific set of customers, understand their problems and underlying causes, and develop a superior solution. If the solution delivers significantly better results than exiting options, the innovator could receive substantial rewards.

For example, pharmaceutical companies develop medicines targeting specific conditions—such as a new cancer treatment—and secure patents. These products or services become highly valuable for a niche customer base, and in cases where no superior alternative exists, customers are willing to pay a premium.

It is important to note that we are not advising on the choice of one goal over another.

If Your Goal Is to Reach the Peak of Mount Everest, Identify Intermediate Destinations along the Way

At times, people set big and ambitious goal—for example, becoming the richest person in the world or the best cricketer in the country. Ideally, we need to establish small, measurable goals to determine the direction and assess our ability to accomplish the ultimate objective. For instance, if you aspire to become the richest person in the world and choose to achieve this through investing, the process will require time. Compounding returns in investing necessitate a reasonable duration to generate favourable outcomes. Additionally, you would need to save money from other income sources and reinvest it constantly to assess whether your strategy is working. Becoming the richest person does not happen overnight.

Hence, it is essential to set measurable goals for shorter durations. Unless you establish small, achievable targets—such as aiming to compound your wealth every five years and reviewing progress at the end of each period—the ultimate goal will remain out of reach.

Similarly, if your goal is to become the best cricketer in the country, you must first establish credibility at important levels, such as district or state competitions. Without proving yourself at these stages, there is no realistic path to reaching the national level. Start by targeting the smallest achievable milestone—such as becoming the best cricketer in your own cricket academy. Once you accomplish that, focus on the next milestone and continue progressing step by step.

Conduct a Gap Assessment

Once you have identified your goal, you need to assess the internal and external factors that may influence your journey towards achieving it. Internal factors include your strengths and weaknesses, while external factors comprise elements beyond your control, such as economic environment and competition.

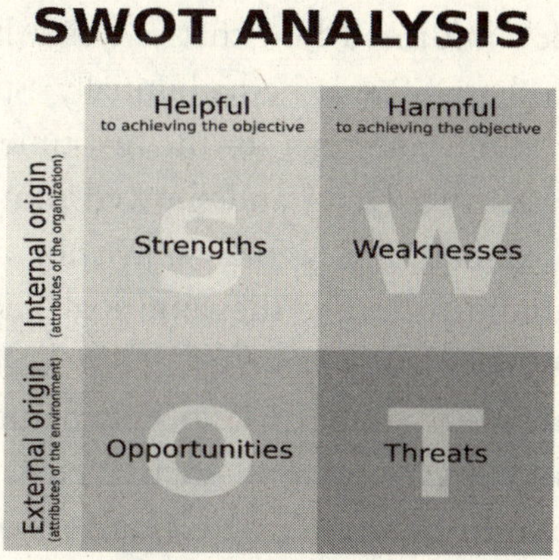

SWOT analysis matrix.
Source: https://en.wikipedia.org/

A SWOT analysis is a simple yet powerful tool used to evaluate strengths, weaknesses, opportunities, and threats:

- **Strengths**: Internal factors that give you an advantage over competitors
- **Weaknesses**: Internal limitations that hinder your performance
- **Opportunities**: External factors that offer potential for growth
- **Threats**: External factors that could negatively impact your business

It may also be valuable to have conversations with both past achievers and those who have struggled on a similar path. Their experience and insights can provide a practical perspective.

Example from the Movie 12th Fail_: Learning from Those Who Have Walked the Path Before_

Manoj decided to become an IPS officer after his friend Pritam Pandey informed him that it was a higher-grade position than the DSP role he had initially aspired to.

Pritam, whom Manoj met for the first time at a railway station, took him to Delhi and showed him the intense competition among IPS aspirants. Manoj realized that millions of candidates shared the same goal, and the success rate was extremely low.

The following morning, Manoj felt demotivated and doubted his ability to achieve such a challenging goal. Pritam then introduced him to Gauri Bhaiya, an IPS aspirant who had attempted the exam multiple times and mentored others based on his past experiences.

Quotation by self-made billionaire Jack Ma.
Source: https://www.cnbc.com/2018/01/30/jack-ma-dont-fear-making-mistakes-in-your-20s-and-30s.html

A key takeaway from this example is that you should not be discouraged by competition or by initial feedback from others. Every individual's journey is unique, and multiple factors influence the ultimate outcome. These factors are discussed in detail later in this book.

Example from 12th Fail*: The Importance of Gap Assessment*

During his IPS exam journey, Manoj successfully cleared the preliminary exam multiple times but struggled with the mains. To understand the reason for his repeated failures, he approached a past IPS exam topper, Deep Mohan, for guidance.

Deep asked Manoj to write an essay within twenty minutes on a seemingly simple topic: 'Manoj Kumar'. Initially, Manoj thought that was an easy exercise and doubted its relevance to his struggles. However, he soon realized that he was unable to write even a single page.

Deep explained that the preliminary exam was a multiple-choice test, whereas the mains exam required candidates to think critically, structure their responses, and write effectively within a limited timeframe. He pointed out that if Manoj found it difficult to write about himself, writing essays on complex topics such as cyber security, governance, and international relations would be even more challenging.

The reality check made Manoj realize his gap skills. He then started reading about current affairs daily, devoted time to practising essay writing, and timed his responses with a stopwatch.

The purpose of gap assessment is to identify areas of weakness and determine the steps needed to bridge the gap.

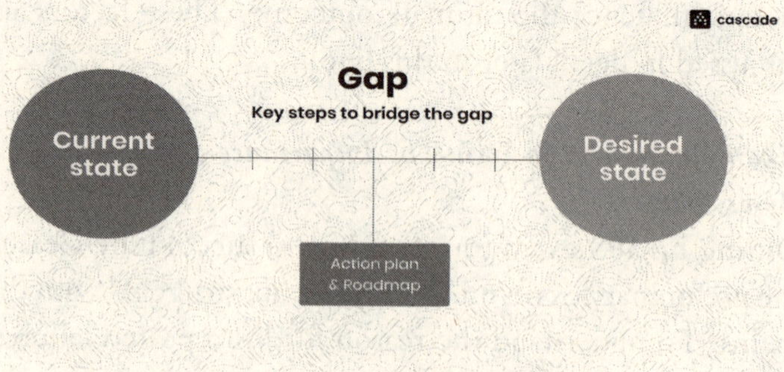

GAP analysis diagram.
Source: https://www.cascade.app/blog/gap-analysis

As highlighted in the example, gap assessment can also be conducted by engaging with people who have successfully achieved similar goals.

By following a structured approach—creating an action plan, staying dedicated, and putting in consistent effort—it is possible to bridge the gap between your current capabilities and the desired skill set.

Gap assessment also helps determine the external support and resources required to reach your goal, such as mentorship, coaching, or financial assistance. For example, if an aspiring entrepreneur lacks capital, such entrepreneur must explore ways to raise funds. However, there may be instances where securing the necessary resources proves challenging.

One last piece of advice—never hesitate to use external resources if they are essential for achieving your goal. Resources can include capital, coaching, mentorship, or other forms of support. In some cases, investing in these resources is not just beneficial but necessary.

Understand what others can offer, how you can leverage those resource, and what you are willing to provide in return. By making strategic use of external support, you can significantly improve your chances of success.

Summary

The journey towards accomplishing a challenging goal begins with selecting the right one. An aspirant must possess both a genuine passion and a clear sense of purpose when striving to achieve a particular objective. The choice should be made only after a holistic evaluation of both internal and external factors.

It is rare for multiple individuals to succeed in the same challenging goal in exactly the same way, making the process of goal selection critically important. A flawed approach at this stage can render the entire investment—of time, energy, resources, and money—futile. Therefore, when identifying a specific goal, it is equally essential to consider alternative options and to understand why each of those was ultimately set aside.

A thorough analysis—including the timing of the opportunity, expected rewards, and a realistic assessment of personal strengths and weaknesses—is essential before committing any effort or resources. Once the decision to pursue a particular goal has been made, the next step is to identify existing gaps and develop an actionable plan to bridge them.

2

Risk and Reward: Managing Uncertainty

We have structured this chapter as follows:

- Risk and rewards go hand in hand: Understanding your risk appetite
- Winners keep taking risks: Outcomes may be unfavourable
- No risk is worth taking if the outcome could leave you bankrupt
- Either you win or you learn: You never truly fail
- The ultimate outcome must be success
- The relationship between risk and age

Risk and Rewards Go Hand in Hand: Understanding Your Risk Appetite

We have used the term 'challenging goal' multiple times in this book. To avoid any confusion, it is important to clarify its meaning. Challenging goals are those that are difficult to accomplish but offer substantial rewards. As mentioned earlier, if one were to conduct a mathematical computation, a challenging goal would have a low probability of success. Therefore, anyone aspiring to achieve a challenging goal must be prepared to take risks in some form.

To discover whether pearls exist in the sea, one must first believe that they do and that they are found within the sea. The next step would be to dive deep to search for them. In this journey, one may encounter sharks and other dangerous species, making the process potentially life-threatening. However, pearls cannot be found by merely observing the sea from the shore. This rarity and difficulty in obtaining them make pearls valuable. Thus, only risk-takers and believers can reap significant rewards.

Without taking the necessary risk, there is no chance of earning substantial rewards—anything beyond a reasonable return or a risk-free return inherently involves some level of risk. As A.P.J. Abdul Kalam once said, 'Man needs difficulties in life because they are necessary to enjoy success.'

Avoiding risk also means losing opportunities. However, whenever possible, it is prudent to assess or compute the risk and reward before committing to a particular risk.

As a frequent derivatives trader, I often experience situations where the risks assumed may exceed or fall short of one's risk tolerance.

It is important to understand your own risk tolerance level or mindset, that is, one should not be lured by the potential returns that could be generated by making a high-risk decision.

A decision involving high risks may indeed offer better rewards. However, such a decision would also entail variability in returns and the potential loss of investment. Therefore, understanding your own risk tolerance level or mindset is crucial.

For example, if a person who struggles to tolerate losses, assumes a high risk—one that would ideally be taken by someone who does not mind losing money—the fluctuations in returns, as well as the potential loss of investment, may have a strong adverse impact on their state of mind and future actions.

Risk tolerance can be increased over time by gradually assuming slightly higher risks. However, taking on a significant amount of high risk in a short period could lead to undesirable exposure.

It is essential to assess your own risk appetite and focus on improving your risk tolerance over time.

Winners Keep Taking Risks: Outcomes May Be Unfavourable

It is important to note that some of the most successful people in the world have taken various risks and have encountered unfavourable outcomes multiple times in their lives.

Berkshire Hathaway's Paytm Investment

According to newspaper reports, Berkshire Hathaway, the investment giant owned by Warren Buffett, sold its entire stake in Paytm in a large block deal, incurring a loss of more than Rs 600 crore, as per stock exchange data.

Berkshire Hathaway had acquired a 2.6 per cent stake in Paytm in 2018, investing nearly Rs 2,200 crore ($300 million), valuing the Vijay Shekhar Sharma-led fintech company at $10–12 billion.

From this stake, Berkshire Hathaway sold 1.56 crore shares, or 2.5 per cent of Paytm's equity, for approximately

Rs 1,370 crore at a share price of Rs 877.29. Additionally, during Paytm's IPO, Berkshire Hathaway sold its remaining shares for Rs 200 crore.

Mukesh Ambani on Embracing Failure

Mukesh Ambani shares from his personal experiences: 'Failures are not setbacks but crucial steps towards eventual success.' He states that out of every ten ventures he has undertaken, he has failed six or seven times but has achieved significant success on three occasions.

For him, entrepreneurs should not be disheartened by failures. Instead, they should embrace them, learn from them, and persevere with resilience and optimism.

The above experiences only outline limited stories of two of the greatest business personalities. However, when you learn about the story of any successful individual, you will realize that they have encountered various failures.

Moreover, the percentage of endeavours in which those individuals have achieved tremendous success is lower than the percentage of endeavours that resulted in average outcomes or failures. Even with years of experience and hard work, setbacks are inevitable.

Various factors influence the outcome of any endeavour, including external elements beyond one's control. Simply put, success is not determined by effort alone. In the long run, failure and setbacks are a natural part of the journey.

Never take failures to heart, and never let them define you. If you have failed or faced a setback, you must continue taking risks in order to succeed next time.

No Risk Is Worth Taking If the Outcome Can Make You Bankrupt

Even if you want to win at a casino (gambling), you need to use your money wisely and in tranches. In life, assuming such a risk is foolish; while it may offer tremendous returns, if the outcomes are unfavourable, you could be left bankrupt (that is, without a second chance).

You can afford to lose only as much as you can later recover. Risk-taking is both a science and an art.

For example, there is an important rule in derivate trading: you cannot lose more than 5 per cent of your capital on a single trade. If you lose more than 5 per cent, you must book the loss immediately. Risking more than 5 per cent of your capital can lead to irreparable damage.

Either You Win or You Learn: You Never Truly Fail

As discussed earlier, it is important to overcome failures and setbacks and keep trying so that the lessons learned from past failures can be better utilized in the future.

In the case of unfavourable outcomes, it is crucial to identify and analyse the reasons behind them and address any gaps to improve future results.

Most of the times, people set challenging goal with enthusiasm and motivation. However, after facing a few setbacks or unfavourable outcomes, they lose confidence and abandon their journey.

When faced with an unfavourable outcome, it is essential to keep trying, as otherwise, the following situations may arise:

- You quit your journey and pursue a simpler, easily achievable goal. However, over time, when you see your peers or friends (who were once part of your journey) achieving similar challenging goals, you may feel a sense of regret. You might wonder, with a little more effort and a further attempt, you could have achieved your goal too.

- You take on another challenging goal. If you start a new challenging pursuit, you may once again face initial setbacks. Constantly jumping from one challenge to another can lead to frustration, anxiety, and even depression, while also resulting in the loss of valuable resources such as time and money.

A.P.J. Abdul Kalam once said: 'When your hopes, dreams, and goals are dashed, search among the wreckage—you may find a golden opportunity hidden in the ruins.'

A combination of the following strategies may be considered when dealing with setbacks on the journey to achieving a challenging goal:

- **Be grateful**: When you encounter a setback, take it as an opportunity to be thankful for the chance to learn, grow, and see things from a different perspective. We know it's not easy to think this way or to absorb a setback, but life is full of failures, obstacles, and challenges. These adversities may redirect you to where you truly should be. They are not throwing you off your path.
- **Avoid blowing a negative situation out of proportion**: Don't let one bad experience cloud your entire outlook.
- **Remember, it is not the end of the road; opportunities will continue to come**: Identify and

analyse the reasons behind the setback. You will have future chances to achieve better results.

- **Regain control and don't lose faith**: Setbacks are often emotional. In many cases, they can (at least temporarily) affect a person's emotional and mental well-being. But you are your own biggest cheerleader. Despite the setback, remember that you are still capable.
- **Consider an alternative path forward**: Exploring a different path doesn't necessarily mean giving up on your goal. Instead, it reflects the idea that there is almost always more than one way to reach your destination. When you experience a setback, one of the best things you can do is to find a way to keep moving forward.

The Ultimate Outcome Must Be Success

To accomplish a challenging goal, your hunger to succeed must be greater than your fear of setbacks.

Example from the Movie 12th Fail

Manoj Kumar, aspiring to become an IPS officer, moved to Delhi with big dreams. During his bus journey, a co-passenger stole all the money he had brought from his village. As a result, Manoj faced severe financial difficulties. To earn a basic living, he worked in a library all day. However, he had to quit that job due to the owner's disrespectful behaviour.

He then took up various jobs—cleaning toilets, working at a tea stall, and operating a gristmill (atta chakki). He did not have enough money to afford essential study resources, including tuition fees.

Despite multiple failures, setbacks, and hardships, he remained determined, continuously working hard, and improving himself. His hunger and ambition drove him to try again and again with full enthusiasm and commitment. The ultimate outcome? He cleared the IPS exam.

The key point is that the journey towards achieving challenging goals is filled with struggles, hardships, and difficult situations. But it is those who are willing to walk the difficult path who ultimately earn the rewards.

A never-give-up attitude is essential for achieving favourable outcomes.

The Relationship between Risk and Age

Starting your journey at an early age comes with a clear advantage—lower opportunity cost. Even if you initially face unfavourable outcomes, you have the benefit of time to change the ultimate outcome.

For instance, starting a business at an early age may be beneficial. Even if the business does not grow in the initial years or incurs losses, the early learning curve can be leveraged later to generate rewards.

Additionally, at a young age, your commitments and responsibilities in other aspects of life are generally fewer. This allows you to adopt an 'all-in' approach (discussed in detail in the next chapter) more freely.

However, if you start at an older age, you may find that your peers have already advanced significantly in their careers. You may also have greater financial commitments and responsibilities, making it more difficult to pursue a challenging goal.

That said, age does not determine one's ability to set and achieve challenging goals—success is possible at both younger and older ages. In fact, older individuals have their own advantages, such as greater life experience and wisdom. Our perspective here focuses on the ability to take risks—younger individuals may have an advantage simply because they have more time to recover from setbacks.

However, whether you are just starting out or are further along in your journey, managing risk thoughtfully—without losing your ambition or becoming paralysed by fear—is essential. In the end, it is not the absence of failure but the persistence through failure that shapes the eventual success story.

3

Essentials for Success: Hard Work, Belief, and Optimism

This chapter is divided into the following sections:

- There is no substitute for hard work
- A positive attitude makes a big difference

There Is No Substitute for Hard Work

A.P.J. Abdul Kalam says, 'If you want to shine like the sun, first burn like the sun.' If you have chosen to pursue a challenging goal, remember that success never comes easily—it requires hard work and dedication.

There are both controllable and uncontrollable factors (discussed in later chapters) that play a critical role in the outcomes of a journey towards accomplishing a challenging goal. In other words, both controllable and uncontrollable factors have a certain impact on the outcome, unless the results are strongly influenced by limited factors (mostly uncontrollable).

Hard work is one of the key controllable differentiating factors compared to others. Knowing that hard work is a controllable factor that can have a favourable impact on the outcome, an aspirant on the journey of achieving a challenging goal should leave no stone unturned when it comes to making efforts in the right direction.

Throughout the journey, one should live by the following principle: whatever you do today will reflect in your future—your actions will determine the outcomes.

Let us look at the journey of a remarkable individual to understand how history can be created through hard work.

The Story of J.K. Rowling (Author of Harry Potter Series)

After many years of struggle, J.K. Rowling was sitting at a train station one day when she randomly pictured a wizard. She quickly jotted down the details and started writing a story.

During this time, she married an abusive husband and eventually got divorced. Because of all the hardships she endured, she suffered from clinical depression and was even suicidal.

After many years, she finally completed the manuscript of her first book, *Harry Potter and the Philosopher's Stone*, but it was rejected by twelve big publishing houses. She did not give up. Finally, a publishing house called Bloomsbury gave her a chance—and today, she is considered one of the most famous authors in the world.

If an aspirant does not put in the required hard work, the outcomes will be significantly influenced by uncontrollable or external factors. Naturally, the probability of success in such cases is much lower compared to a situation where the aspirant makes every possible effort to influence the outcomes.

A.P.J. Abdul Kalam once said, 'God helps only those who work hard. That principle is very clear.' Additionally, it is crucial to understand that, in the long term, the ultimate outcome will never be favourable without the required hard work.

At times, in the short term, certain external factors—such as luck, favouritism, or third-party influence—may play a role in delivering beneficial outcomes. However, these factors alone are not sufficient to help one reach the ultimate goal or destination.

Real-Life Example: The Perils of Complacency in Leadership and Business

Mr A was the son of a successful business tycoon. Upon his father's retirement, Mr A inherited his father's stake in the company, ABC Limited, and was also appointed CEO. However, his appointment was not straightforward. The existing investors preferred the deputy CEO, Mr B, for the role, given his twenty-five years of experience in the organization. Mr B had closely observed the company's growth and was involved in most strategic decisions.

To secure Mr A's nomination, his father had to personally persuade the investors, arguing that Mr A would be the best choice for the company. He highlighted that Mr A had a qualification from a top business school—something neither his father nor Mr B had. Furthermore, Mr A had a larger stake in the company, whereas Mr B only held ESOPs granted to him over the years.

A year later, Mr B left the company to start his own business in the same category, focusing on leveraging technology to run operations.

At the time of Mr A's succession, ABC Limited was the market leader in its category—retail fashion and grocery through company-owned and company-opened (COCO) stores. The next-biggest player had only half of ABC Limited's market share.

For the first few years, ABC Limited continued to perform well, benefiting from its market dominance and years of brand-building. Mr A's father, who was unwell, frequently warned him, 'We are at the peak of the business cycle. We need to leverage technology and shift our business model.' One day, the father passed away from natural causes.

Meanwhile, Mr B had been growing his online business, successfully influencing consumer behaviour. His company offered significantly lower prices due to minimal operational costs.

During regular board meetings, the investors repeatedly urged Mr A to adapt to the changing market—or risk being replaced. However, Mr A was more focused on his luxurious lifestyle and frequent holidays. He believed the business would continue generating income with little effort, even if profits were declining.

The company needed a leader with the drive and ability to adapt to market shifts—not someone content in his comfort zone.

Mr A visited the office only once a week for three hours, merely to receive updates. The team leaders helped present a favourable picture at board meetings and were rewarded by Mr A during performance appraisals for their loyalty.

Whenever investors proposed a resolution to change the CEO, Mr A blocked it, leveraging his significant ownership in the company. Eventually, the investors sought and obtained a waiver from Mr A to invest in Mr B's new-age business. They began diverting funds towards Mr B's company instead.

In the next three years, the story unfolded as follows:

- The investors passed a resolution to remove Mr A as CEO and replace him with an investor-nominated director, citing negligence, fraud, and other relevant clauses under the shareholders' agreement.
- Meanwhile, Mr B's company flourished. Seeing its immense potential, the investors exercised their drag-along rights to merge ABC Limited with Mr B's company.
- Mr B was able to raise funds at an increasingly high valuation, while ABC Limited struggled to attract buyers. As a result, the merger took place at a discounted valuation. The justification was that Mr B's company had strong growth potential, whereas ABC Limited's assets lacked competitive appeal.
- Mr A fell into depression. With no successor to turn to for support, he ultimately succumbed to cancer.

Mr A had everything—except the willingness to put in the hard work needed to take the business to new heights. Success is not guaranteed by privilege, inheritance, or external support. Hard work is the defining factor that determines whether one can sustain and grow their achievements. There truly is no substitute for hard work.

A Positive Attitude Makes a Big Difference

Success seems elusive when you are consumed by anxieties, doubts, and self-destructive habits. To accomplish a challenging goal, an aspirant needs strong self-belief and optimism. Self-belief means having faith and confidence in your ability to achieve your goal, whereas optimism is the ability to focus on and leverage favourable factors without being mentally demotivated by negative ones.

An aspirant should not dwell on the fact that only a small percentage of people eventually succeed in accomplishing challenging goals. Instead, they should take comfort in knowing that success is still achievable and that they can be part of that successful group.

Visualize the moment of success—when only a small percentage of people succeed, and you are one of them. That feeling can be immensely satisfying and provide the motivation needed to overcome challenges.

The important question to ask yourself is: Why can't I be a part of that successful percentage? Everyone has the same eyes, legs, hands, and ears. If everyone starts on an equal footing, why not focus on what is needed to accomplish the goal?

Real-Life Example: Overcoming Doubt with Confidence and Determination

When I (Anuj) was pursuing CA, I once met a very senior person who asked me, 'What are you doing for your career?'

I answered, 'I'm doing CA.'

He responded, 'Does everyone really qualify? Let's see if you will.'

I was angry at his unwarranted reaction. However, I asked myself, 'What would stop me from becoming a CA?'

I was putting in my best effort. I was confident that I could do it. Even if only a small fraction of people eventually qualifies, I knew I could be part of that group. I resolved to do whatever was necessary to achieve my goal. Try to look at the positive side and be happy with what the life has offered to you.

Mukesh Ambani's Tip for Entrepreneurs

'The entrepreneur is an optimist. There are a lot of cynics and people who think negatively. Glass half full, never half empty,' he said.

Ambani believes that entrepreneurs must embody optimism, resisting negativity and cynicism. Adopting a 'glass half full' mentality is essential for navigating uncertainties and capitalizing on opportunities.

A.P.J. Abdul Kalam once said, 'All birds find shelter during a rain. But the eagle avoids rain by flying above the clouds. Problems are common, but attitude makes the difference.'

In a nutshell, the following key strategies may be considered for building optimism:

- **Build self-belief and confidence in your capabilities**: You must first believe that what you aspire to achieve is truly within your reach. As discussed above, an aspirant should not dwell on the fact that only a small percentage of people ultimately succeed in accomplishing a challenging goal. It is equally important to work hard—to the best of your abilities—to build genuine confidence in your capabilities. So, develop self-belief and work diligently, so you can face difficult challenges with assurance.

- **Focus on the positives**: As mentioned earlier, a positive attitude can make a significant difference. With a positive mindset, one can handle difficult problems more effectively. A person with a positive attitude is better equipped to spot opportunities in challenging situations and to disregard the inevitable obstacles that arise in the process of overcoming them.
- **Have faith that you will identify controllable factors in difficult situations**: In challenging scenarios, it is crucial to identify controllable factors as early as possible. Difficult situations often involve numerous uncontrollable factors, which can make them seem overwhelming. The aspirant must have faith that they will be able to identify the controllable aspects of a complex problem and, in doing so, eventually find a way forward.

4

Decide and Start: From Dream to Action

'If you have built castles in the air, your work need not be lost; that is where they should be. Now put the foundations under them.'

—Henry David Thoreau

We will divide this discussion into the following parts:

- Outcomes (whether good or bad) can only be observed when you make a decision and start the journey.
- If you do not start, the only outcome is the regret of an opportunity not pursued.
- In case of confusion, assess whether there is any potential loss in making a decision and starting the journey—and whether you are willing to accept that loss, if any.

Outcomes (Whether Good or Bad) Can Only Be Observed When You Make a Decision and Start the Journey

No matter how good or bad an idea may seem, without execution, you will never truly know the outcomes. If you have thought through an idea, it is important to make a decision and work towards its execution. Even if the idea is not unique, execution can sometimes make a significant difference.

Take the example of any successful founder who has created an unconventional business (such as Facebook, WhatsApp, Tinder, Zomato). Initially, they had no way of knowing whether their idea would grow to a large business. Therefore, outcomes—whether good or bad—can only be observed and improved upon when you make a decision and start the journey.

If You Do Not Start, the Only Outcome Is the Regret of an Opportunity Not Pursued

Real-Life Example: Missed Opportunities and the Cost of Inaction

I (Anuj) moved from Jaipur to Gurgaon to pursue my professional career after completing CA and CS. I had to take up a job, and Gurgaon was the best option, as it was close to my hometown.

In the initial years, my salary was modest, so I had to stay in shared accommodations or paying guest houses. In such arrangements, the food was often subpar in both taste and quality.

After working for ten to fourteen hours a day, food becomes an essential need—one that no one wants to compromise on. After living in Gurgaon for a few years, I had a business idea. I realized that in cities like Gurgaon, there are many migrants who stay in shared accommodations because of the high rent. I thought it might be a good idea to create a platform that connects tenants with freelancers who can cook food.

This would not only provide employment opportunities for people migrating from smaller cities but also offer a solution to working professionals in need of quality home-cooked meals.

Over time, we could introduce add-ons such as catering services for parties and sourcing cooking materials and spices from our own warehouses.

The next step was to build a prototype of the business, such as a tech platform, and test the market response. However, I was not from a technology background, and I did not take the initiative to find a co-founder. I feared that if I shared my idea with someone from a tech background, they might start the business on their own.

Ultimately, I did nothing about the idea. Years later, I read newspaper articles about startups and large e-commerce players pursuing a similar concept—not just in India but also in Canada, the UK, and other countries. At that moment, all I felt was the regret of missing an opportunity I could have pursued.

Evaluate Potential Losses before Starting the Journey

Many times, people feel bad when they see others achieving challenging goals and regret that they, too, could have done the same. A better approach is to recognize your aspiration, make a decision, and take action.

If you are struggling to decide, think about the worst-case scenario. Would there be any real loss in making a decision and starting the journey? Even if there is a potential loss, are you willing to accept it?

At worst, you may have to invest some money, time, and other resources. However, in return, you will at least gain some valuable learning and perhaps a reality check. Then, whatever you do next, you will have better clarity.

Real-Life Example: Gaining Clarity through Exploration and Self-Reflection

After completing my (Anuj) CA and CS qualifications, I was working in a reputed global MNC in a highly specialized field—M&A tax.

I realized that I wanted to pursue an MBA, as it would expand my career opportunities (including roles in management consulting, investment banking, private equity, and strategic management) and could provide a favourable long-term career path.

I started preparing for the GMAT (MBA entrance exam). My math skills were strong, so my GMAT quantitative score was excellent. However, my verbal score was not great, which impacted my overall GMAT score.

I spent a few months improving my verbal skills but was unable to make a significant difference. I studied over weekends and attended virtual GMAT classes.

While speaking with MBA alumni and gathering insights, I realized that top-tier management consulting firms, investment banks, and private equity funds typically recruit students with outstanding academic records or highly relevant experience.

I asked myself, given my purpose for pursuing an MBA, did my entrance score align with my career goals? The answer was that the entrance scores generally indicate a candidate's potential performance in the programme. Did my academic record demonstrate an exceptional track record? No. While my academic background was strong, it may not have been competitive enough for my dream roles. Would an MBA truly transform my career in just one year?

In the end, the only things I lost by preparing for the GMAT were money and time. However, I gained much-needed clarity—I realized I should continue in my current role and focus on the opportunities that came my way.

Looking back, the decision has worked out well. At least now, I will not regret missing the opportunity to do an MBA from a top business school and enter management consulting, investment banking, private equity, or strategic management.

I tried, and I now understand that it was not the right path for me.

Key takeaways from the above example:

- If you have a dream to pursue a particular challenging goal (which you would have chosen after the appropriate analysis outlined in Chapter 1), it is always a sound decision to invest the required time and resources. The early outcomes of your investment will help you identify your shortcomings—areas that need improvement—in order to attain the desired results. Alternatively, you may decide not to pursue the goal further.
- Be willing to accept potential loss: In a worst-case scenario, you may end up losing time and money. It is important to understand that the loss of resources—including time and money—is often necessary cost of trying something new in the pursuit of favourable outcomes.
- Take a leap of faith and begin the journey: Once you have made a decision, you must commit yourself fully

to achieving the goal. Even if the outcomes do not meet expectations—due to various factors, both controllable and uncontrollable—you will still have gained valuable experience from the investment of your time and resources. Unless you actually walk a particular path, there is no better way to predict the eventual outcome.

5

Go All In: Total Commitment to Your Goal

If you want something badly enough, you'll find a way to make it happen.

We have divided this discussion into the following parts:

- Outcomes could be adverse when multiple goals are pursued simultaneously
- A one-pointed approach with complete devotion
- Ways to cultivate devotion towards a goal
- There is no point in making a half-hearted effort

Outcomes Could Be Adverse When Multiple Goals Are Pursued Simultaneously

Many times, we observe people pursuing multiple goals simultaneously—not due to financial commitments or responsibilities, but perhaps because they believe that diversifying their efforts reduces risk, that is, they assume they will achieve at least one of their goals.

However, one must understand that challenging goals demand complete dedication, hard work, commitment, and investment (both in terms of time and money).

Large corporates may be able to pursue multiple goals simultaneously, given their adequate resources and dedicated workforce to drive each agenda. However, for an individual, it may be impossible to pursue multiple challenging goals at the same time. The likelihood of adverse outcomes across all goals is much higher unless the goals overlap significantly.

Given the intense competition, time commitment, and obstacles along the way, unless one is completely dedicated and loyal to a particular goal, the chances of failures increase significantly. To increase the chances of successfully accomplishing a challenging goal, one must be wholly devoted—body, mind, and soul—focusing entirely on a single objective.

In practical terms, there may be unavoidable situations where pursuing multiple goals is necessary. However, for this discussion, let's not focus on such cases.

***Example from the Movie* M.S. Dhoni: The Untold Story**

Mahi was selected for the Ranji Trophy, but his notice was delayed, causing him to arrive late in Kolkata despite his friends' efforts to help.

To please his father, he took up a job as a ticket collector at Kharagpur railway station. However, over time, he became disheartened with his work. Encouraged by his manager, Mahi decided to continue playing cricket alongside his job, practising after his day shifts.

He participated in various tournaments and was eventually selected for the Railways team. After delivering strong performances, he tried out for the Indian national under-19 cricket team. Unfortunately, Bihar lost to

Punjab, where Yuvraj Singh scored 301 runs, and Mahi was not selected—though he did secure a spot in the Duleep Trophy.

Later, Mahi left his job and admitted to his father that cricket was his only ambition. He worked hard, earned his place in the national team, and eventually made his debut.

A One-Pointed Approach with Complete Devotion

As discussed earlier, outcomes may be adverse when multiple goals are pursued simultaneously.

It is therefore important to understand the benefits of focusing on one challenging goal at a time—that is, adopting a one-pointed approach with complete devotion.

In a speech, Mr Mukesh Ambani shared a thought by Swami Vivekananda that, he said, had inspired him throughout his life. He quoted: 'Swami Vivekananda said, "Take up one idea. Make that one idea your life; dream of it; think of it; live on that idea. Let the brain, the body, muscles, nerves, every part of your body be full of that idea, and just leave every other idea alone. This is the way to success."'

Similarly, A.P.J. Abdul Kalam stated, 'To succeed in your mission, you must have single-minded devotion to your goal.'

As mentioned earlier, complete devotion means treating an idea or goal as though it were the sole purpose of your existence on this earth.

There is no other ambition or objective you wish to pursue—no second, third, or any number of alternative choices in life. With such devotion, you would do everything in your power to accomplish your chosen goal.

Even if the chances of success were slim, this level of commitment would compel you to exhaust every possible effort to improve those odds and ultimately achieve success.

Ways to Cultivate Devotion towards a Goal

Below are various ways to help cultivate devotion towards a goal:

Respect Your Goal

If you don't make your dreams the most important thing in your life, who will? It is your responsibility to understand what your goal means to you. When you are devoted to something, it is usually because you find meaning and purpose in it. Take time to reflect on why you are pursuing a particular goal and what it truly means to you.

Your goal must be your top priority in life. You need to have a deep conviction that the purpose of your life is to accomplish the goal you have chosen.

Create Commitment

You need to develop a deep relationship with your goal. There are only two ways this relationship will end: either you accomplish it, or you die. Here, the 'dying' part is used metaphorically to describe a situation where an unfortunate event beyond your control prevents you from achieving your goal. Until then, you must not stop.

It is easy to have the will or motivation to succeed, but desire alone will not get you anywhere unless you take the necessary steps to reach your goal. Without a firm decision to commit, your desire remains just a wish.

Art Turock says, 'There's a difference between interest and commitment. When you're interested in doing something, you do it only when circumstances permit. When you're committed to something, you accept no excuses, only results.'

Listen to Your Heart

Due to the power of human emotions, feelings are often considered far stronger than thoughts and, therefore, have a greater impact on actions.

You may feel exhausted and discouraged by failures, but if your heart tells you to keep going, you will. Follow your heart, and in times of crisis, ask yourself one question: 'If I give up now, if I let my goals disappear, will I be okay with that?'

Steve Jobs says, 'Have the courage to follow your heart and intuition. They somehow know what you truly want to become.'

Reduce Distractions and Clarify Your Priorities

The world is full of distractions, with countless things vying for your attention—but not everything is worth doing. The first step is to identify the activities that are critical for achieving your goal and determine the right timing for them.

The most important task is to prioritize and focus only on what truly matters for accomplishing your goal. Everything else should take lower priority.

There Is No Point in Making a Half-Hearted Effort

If you are required to pursue multiple goals at the same time, whether intentionally or unintentionally, your devotion and effort towards each of them can never be equal. From the very beginning, one thing is clear: you will either accomplish one of those goals or none at all.

If you are likely to achieve only one challenging goal out of many, it is wiser to make a well-informed decision from the outset and choose a single goal to focus on. Once you achieve that goal, other goals may lose their relevance, as you would naturally shift your attention to the growth and furtherance of your accomplishment.

As discussed earlier, when choosing to pursue multiple challenging goals, there is often an inherent belief that the chances of succeeding in at least one will be higher. However, given the complexities involved in achieving each goal, there is also a strong possibility that none will be accomplished due to a lack of devotion, commitment, and the necessary focus to perform the required tasks.

Additionally, when you face setbacks in one journey, you may abandon it and shift focus to another goal, only to later realize that every goal has its own challenges. Had you been pursuing just one challenging goal, the strategies for overcoming setbacks (as discussed in this book) could have been applied more effectively, leading to better outcomes.

If you choose a single goal and it means everything to you, you will eventually find ways to achieve it. Simply put, conserving effort and resources—rather than spreading them across multiple goals—ensures that they are fully directed towards accomplishing one goal.

Real-Life Example: The Risks of Divided Focus in Entrepreneurship

Mr A was keen to start his own business and was convinced by two business ideas: launching a marketplace platform and setting up a derivative trading firm.

Coming from a technology background, he began working on both businesses simultaneously. Since he could not devote himself fully to either, he brought in co-founders—one with a sales and marketing background for the marketplace platform and another, a data scientist, for the derivative trading firm.

To raise capital for both businesses, he engaged an investment banker. However, when the banker discovered that Mr A was involved in two ventures at once, he flagged it as a concern. Despite this, driven by the potential success fee, the banker took on both mandates. Based on his market knowledge, though, he focused primarily on raising funds for the marketplace business.

With the investment banker's support, Mr A pitched the marketplace business idea to multiple investors and successfully secured funding from a reputed investor. However, his co-founder from the marketplace platform later accepted a leadership role at a global MNC and left the business.

Since no funds could be raised for the derivative trading firm, Mr A invested his personal savings into it. When his marketplace co-founder departed, he had to devote more time to that business. At the same time, he lost his invested capital in the derivative trading firm due to an incorrect trading decision made by his other co-founder, leading to the eventual closure of the firm.

Had he invested that capital into the marketplace business instead, he would have secured a larger stake alongside the other investors. However, since his personal capital was tied to the derivative trading firm, he remained emotionally and financially committed to it, diverting time and effort away from the marketplace business.

Even after securing funding for the marketplace platform, investors imposed restriction on fund utilization due to the absence of a co-founder or business leader with strategic expertise in sales and marketing. Despite hiring external employees to drive the business, the outcomes were unfavourable. Ultimately, investors saw no monetary reward and decided to discontinue the marketplace business, triggering the liquidation clause to withdraw their investment.

This scenario highlights the importance of focusing on a single goal at a time. Had Mr A chosen to pursue only one business—either the derivative trading firm or the marketplace platform—his chances of success could have been better. If he had chosen the marketplace business, he should have focused on developing his own sales and marketing skills instead of relying on external support.

6

Control Your Emotions: Stay Focused

In this chapter, we will discuss key emotional challenges that one may generally encounter on the journey to accomplishing a challenging goal:

- People may laugh at you and question your capabilities.
- You may need to walk alone—your close family members and friends may not accompany you or act on your behalf.
- Social pressure.
- Peer pressure.
- Managing separations and adverse events.
- Setbacks (which we have already discussed in detail in Chapter 3).

This is not exhaustive; there may be several other emotional challenges one must deal with throughout the journey.

A key quality that an aspirant should develop to navigate emotional difficulties is the ability to 'identify and focus only on conversations that are relevant while learning to ignore those that should not matter'. People may say things to break you down emotionally. Learning to filter out such negativity is essential.

Let's discuss this in detail.

People May Laugh at You and Question Your Capabilities

Example from the Movie* 83 *(The Story of India's Incredible Cricket World Cup Victory in 1983)

Before the commencement of the 1983 Cricket World Cup, Kapil Dev attended a press conference. A well-known journalist asked him, 'What do you think are India's chances of winning the World Cup?'

Kapil Dev replied, 'We are here to win.'

The reporter smiled and, with a surprised expression, asked, 'You mean to win the World Cup?'

Kapil Dev, maintaining a composed demeanour, responded, 'What else are we here for?'

The best way to deal with laughter and scepticism is to visualize your destination. Imagine the moment when you will achieve your goal and the immense satisfaction it will bring, and then continue your hard work.

There is no point in reacting or feeling bad about people's laughter or doubts. Opinions have no bearing on the final outcome. It is natural to feel hurt, but discipline yourself to refrain from reacting. Instead, whenever you get a moment of reflection, reaffirm your goal as discussed above. Reacting in anger or frustration only expresses your emotions, but if you fail, those same people will laugh even more, believing they were right all alone.

However, if you succeed, your achievements will speak for themselves—leaving no room for further scepticism. The very people who once doubted or mocked you will eventually respect you, provided you have not responded with anger or aggression.

A moment of laughter or a sceptical remark may bring temporary amusement to some, but let them have it. Your success will provide them with the ultimate answer—for a lifetime.

Jennette Winterson says, 'Of course, people will laugh at you, but people laugh at great many things so there is no need to take it personally.'

You May Need to Walk Alone—Your Close Family Members and Friends May Not Accompany You or Act on Your Behalf

If you have decided to pursue a challenging goal, always remember that you will need to walk alone. At times, you may experience deep loneliness during the journey. However, as you progress, you will gradually build resilience against this emotion.

Real-Life Example: Adapting to Change and Building Resilience

Mr A, a twenty-one-year-old college graduate, lived in a small town in Haryana. He was keen to become a top leader in the national army. To pursue his goal, he relocated from his hometown to New Delhi and joined a training academy to prepare for admission into the army.

Back home, he used to spend time daily with his school and college friends, and family members. However, at the training academy, only trainees, trainers, and staff were allowed to stay on campus. Family members and friends were permitted to visit only once a month for a one-hour duration.

Initially, adapting to this change was difficult for Mr A. He felt lonely. At times, he considered quitting the training, returning home, and starting a small business with his friends.

However, over time, he learned to cope with being away from his family and old friends. He built new friendships at the training academy, which helped him manage his loneliness.

Upon completing his training, Mr A was posted to a strategic border location. His new friends from the academy were assigned to different locations as per operational requirements. Once again, he experienced loneliness.

Over the years, he gradually adapted to being away from his close family and friends. Initially, he spent thirty minutes daily with a new friend, playing and chatting in the evenings. Within a month, he had built strong new friendships at his posting.

For the next five years, his posting location changed frequently. Eventually, he stopped forming deep attachments to people. While he continued making new friends and maintaining relationships, by the third year of his service, he had become comfortable with changing location and meeting new people.

Certain emotions are difficult to manage at first, but with time, individuals learn to cope. It is essential to face these emotions and challenging situations to build resilience.

Social Pressure

People often have a habit of comparing things—and sometimes, they extend this habit to comparing individuals.

Some groups of people exhibit this tendency more than others.

As we discussed earlier, in the long run, only a small group of people will achieve challenging goals. Additionally, as explored in previous chapters, everyone follows their own unique journey, influenced by multiple factors.

We have also established that risk and reward go hand in hand, and not everyone assume equal or similar risks. Therefore, while an aspirant should consider others' opinions, the ultimate decisions must be made independently.

A person's past experiences significantly shape their opinions. Hence, anyone aspiring to achieve a challenging goal must assess their own risk appetite, consider fallback scenarios (as a worst-case plan), and be emotionally prepared to stand by their decision.

Example from the Movie **Gully Boy**

Gully Boy is a film about a twenty-two-year-old boy, Murad. He was the son of a driver, and his parents worked hard to educate him so he could secure a white-collar job. However, Murad realized his true passion—becoming a rapper.

After a heated argument with his father, Murad decided to leave home and live independently. His mother supported his decision and moved with him.

One day, Murad's father visited him after learning that he had quit his job to pursue his dream. Murad's father confronted him: 'Look at your background. Where do you come from? What resources do you have? Right now, I am struggling to afford even the basic necessities. People from such a background cannot make big decisions like this. You should apologize to your boss and go back to work.'

Murad responded: 'Your thoughts are shaped by your experiences, and they may be valid for you—but they may not be true for everyone.'

His father insisted, 'People should have dreams that align with their reality.'

However, Murad was determined. He replied, 'I will change my reality to match my dreams. I will honour the gift that God has given me and become a successful rapper.'

The key takeaway is this: People may disagree with your approach or hold different views, but your decision is yours alone.

We often encounter situations where people make decisions based on the advice of others—whether from parents, seniors, or mentors—and later blame them if things don't go as planned.

Always remember, there is no point in blaming others for the decisions you made. You sought guidance, and they only tried to help you. At the end of the day, you always have your own mind to make your own decisions.

Peer pressure

Peer pressure arises when an individual is not entirely convinced about their chosen path or life direction but continues in that direction simply to keep up with their peer group.

Additionally, aspirants may experience peer pressure when they observe their competitors succeeding, leading them to question their own decisions or adjust their course based on others' outcomes. For example, Mr A was an aspiring entrepreneur who was building a startup. He noticed that his batchmates and friends—who were also working on their startups—had successfully raised funds. Meanwhile, Mr A was struggling to secure capital. Naturally, this created a sense of peer pressure.

However, as we have discussed repeatedly, ultimate success depends on multiple factors coming together, many of which will be explored in the later chapters of this book.

If your peers are currently ahead of you, trust that your time will come. Opportunities will arise for you as well—be patient and ensure that you fully capitalize on them when they do.

Jeff Moore says, 'You would have no peer pressure if you cared less about the opinion of others.'

Managing Separations and Adverse Events

As discussed earlier, your decision to pursue a particular goal should not depend on others accompanying you on that journey, because when you reach the peak, you may find yourself alone.

That said, having a companion or support system—such as a close friend or family member can be highly beneficial. Such companionship can provide energy and encouragement to help you navigate difficulties.

However, one must be mindful that separation from such a companion during the journey can be emotionally devastating and difficult to cope with.

There may also be times when adverse events—such as an accident or the loss of a loved one—occur. These can be physically and mentally overwhelming, significantly impacting your ability to move forward.

In such situations:

- If necessary, take a break, but do not lose sight of your destination.
- Keep visualizing your goal—remind yourself why you started.
- Remember that every phase will pass with time—time is the greatest healer of many pains.

In the end, you cannot abandon your goal—you must push forward and reach your destination.

7

Plan before Execution: Strategy for Success

'A good plan is like a road map: it shows the final destination and usually the best way to get there.'

—H. Stanely Judd

This discussion is divided into the following sections:

- Execution without a plan increases the risk of failure
- Make both long-term and short-term plans
- Track performance against the plan and keep refining it
- Identify the reason for gaps between your plan and actual results

Execution without a Plan Increase the Risk of Failure

'Give me six hours to chop down a tree, and I will spend the first four sharpening the axe.'

—Abraham Lincoln

Real-Life Example: The Importance of Planning for a Successful Outcome

Let's take a simple real-life situation—say, you want to go on a vacation. As soon as that desire arises, the following basic questions ideally come to mind:

- Who will be on the vacation with you—perhaps a friend or family—or will it be a solo trip?
- What type of location would you prefer?
- What is your total budget?
- How many days do you have for the trip?
- Do you have any destination on your bucket list?
- Is it peak season for the destinations on your bucket list?
- Are there any other considerations, such as vegetarian food or travel-related challenges?

Based on these questions, you make a decision. Now, let us hypothetically assume the answers to some of these questions:

- It will be a solo trip.
- You prefer a location with beaches, islands, and parties.
- Rs 40,000 is a reasonable budget, with a 15 per cent buffer.
- You can spare seven days—anything beyond that is not possible due to professional commitments.
- Yes, it will be peak season (say, you plan to go in December).
- You need vegetarian food only.

Recently, on social media, you have noticed that many people travel to Thailand for vacations. Based on this, you decide to visit Thailand. Once you have chosen Thailand as your destination, in an ideal scenario:

- You would plan where to visit in Thailand (for example, Koh Phangan for a Full Moon Party, Phuket for its nightlife, etc.).

- Based on factors such as budget, duration, and departure/arrival times, you would finalize the mode of transport between locations.
- Similarly, considering your budget, accessibility, and food availability, you would decide on the type and location of your stay.

Then, you would create a complete itinerary (which you may or may not modify later). Based on your itinerary, you would make bookings in advance to avoid any hassles and naturally follow the plan during your trip.

Now, let's assume the trip was not planned as above—there was no itinerary, and decisions were made randomly. What would happen?

- You book your tickets and arrive in Thailand (say, Bangkok). You spend Rs 12,000 on a one-way flight and Rs 6,000 on a single-entry visa.
- You book a one-night stay near the airport in Bangkok for Rs 6,000.
- You take cabs to travel within Bangkok.
- At the last minute, you book a flight to Phuket for Rs 10,000.
- The next morning, you run out of budget and realize that Rs 46,000 is not sufficient for this trip.
- Since you are short on money, you can no longer afford basic activities like island trips and parties.
- You cannot afford to travel to Koh Phangan for your dream Full Moon Party.
- All you can manage is a two-night stay in Phuket (Rs 6,000 for two nights in an affordable hotel) and a return ticket to India (Rs 10,000).

Had you planned the trip properly or consulted a travel planner, you could have managed this trip within a budget of Rs 50,000.

The purpose of this example is to illustrate how even simple desires or goals can lead to negative outcomes without a properly planned approach. See how a simple vacation, when unplanned, resulted in failure?

A Goal without a Plan Is Just a Wish

After going through this example, it is worth considering: how can challenging goals have favourable outcomes without a well-planned approach? Execution without planning means heading in an arbitrary direction. Such an approach is acceptable only if the individual is making a half-hearted effort and has no real concern for the outcome. To succeed in any challenging goal, you need a well-structured plan.

> *'For every minute spent in organizing, an hour is earned.'*
> —Benjamin Franklin

Make Both Long-Term and Short-Term Plans

> *Small actions over shorter time frames generate bigger outcomes over the long term—the Taj Mahal took twenty-two years to be completed.*

Achieving a challenging goal takes months or even years. Hence, in addition to defining a long-term plan, it is equally important to identify short-term plans—actionable steps for a day, a week, or more. The achievement of long-term goals is highly dependent on the successful execution of short-term plans.

> *'You can't produce a baby in one month by getting nine women pregnant.'*
>
> —Warren Buffett

Accomplishing a long-term goal usually take several years, as such goals represent significant achievements or milestones.

In contrast, short-term plans are objectives that can be achieved in the near future—typically within a few weeks, months, or up to a year.

Short-term plans serve as stepping stones towards larger goals, helping to track progress, and providing immediate focus and motivation for daily actions.

Track Performance against the Plan and Keep Refining It

Once you have a long-term plan and short-term actionable (the building blocks of a larger goal), you should begin execution based on the plan. Your plan may evolve over time, but you must track your progress periodically against the predefined plan and identify any gaps.

There will inevitably be situations where actual performance does not align with the plan. To bridge the gap between the plan and actual performance, the plan must be refined and improved regularly.

Identify the Reasons for Gaps between Your Plan and Actual Results

As discussed earlier, there will always be instances where gaps exist between the plan and actual performance. However, identifying the reasons for these gaps is crucial. Without understanding the cause, neither the plan nor actual performance can be improved.

Real-Life Example: Strategic Planning and Adaptability in Exam Preparation

When I (Anuj) was pursuing my CA course, I had to clear the Foundation Test (CPT), followed by the Intermediate level (IPCC) exam. Upon completing IPCC, I had to undergo a three-year internship before taking the CA final exam.

After two and a half years of internship, there was a five- to six-month study break allotted for CA final exam preparation. Similarly, I received a five-month leave to prepare for my CA final exam. As soon as my leave began, I took a week-long holiday to Goa.

Upon returning, I bought a diary and spent an entire day planning how I would use the next five months—essentially creating a vision for my preparation period. I started by answering the following questions:

- How many days should I allocate to each subject?
- Which subject should I complete first, and which should be left for last?
  - I decided to start with problem-solving subjects (accounting, costing, financial management) and later tackle subjects requiring more memory retention.
- How much time should I set aside for mock tests and revisions?

Once I determined the sequence of subjects and the number of days required for each, the next step was to break down my daily study targets—such as the number of pages, questions, or chapters to be covered. Based on this exercise, I developed a structured plan for three to four months, reserving the final month for mock tests and revisions. With the plan in place, I proceeded to execute it.

While drafting my five-month plan, I ensured it was realistic by including time for various activities: one hour for the gym, one hour for my favourite TV show, and one hour for socializing with friends.

However, unexpected challenges arose along the way, which required adjustments:

- Lack of initial efficiency: I struggled to study for eight to ten hours straight, as I was not accustomed to such intense preparation.
- Unexpected guests: Some guests arrived at our house and stayed for a few days.
- Family emergency: A close family member faced an emergency, forcing me to pause my studies for seven days.
- Family functions: Attending wedding and family outings were unavoidable.

To manage these disruptions, I revised my plan weekly to compensate for any lost study time.

After completing my first round of preparation (about four months), I attempted mock test papers—only to realize that my preparation felt inadequate. At this stage, I analysed my performance and identified key gaps. While reviewing the auditing mock test paper, I realized this subject posed a serious threat to my goal of passing CA on my first attempt.

I allocated the next fifteen days to strengthening my grasp of auditing. During this period, I reviewed all available virtual classes on auditing and prepared concise summary notes for last-minute revision. By then, only one month remained. While I had successfully addressed my weak auditing preparation, I needed to ensure the remaining seven subjects were thoroughly revised.

I created a revised one-month plan, ensuring all remaining gaps were closed. Additionally, I developed a strategy for revising each subject in the one-day break before each exam—preparing summary notes for quick reference.

Key takeaways from this example:

- A written plan is essential for achieving long-term goals.
- External challenges and unforeseen situations will arise, requiring continuous plan adjustments.
- Gaps between the plan and actual performance are inevitable, but having a plan helps track and manage them.
- If a significant shortcoming is identified, the plan must be reworked entirely.
- Keep refining the plan based on real-time experiences and learnings.

Summary

Key takeaways from this chapter are outlined below:

- The accomplishment of a challenging goal is impossible without a proper plan (roadmap). It is difficult to achieve even a simple or easily attainable goal without planning—so attempting to reach a challenging goal without a structured approach is nearly impossible. An unplanned effort to accomplish such a goal will almost certainly lead to negative outcomes, including wasted time and resources.

- Execution without planning means heading in an arbitrary direction. Such an approach is acceptable only when the individual is making a half-hearted effort and is unconcerned about the outcome.
- In addition to long-term plans, it is equally important to have short-term plans. Short-term plans serve as stepping stones towards a larger goal and help track progress. They also provide areas of immediate focus and offer motivation for daily actions.
- Plans keep changing over time, while goals remain the same. There will inevitably be situations where actual performance does not align with the plan. To bridge the gap between planned and actual outcomes, plans must be refined and improved regularly. Identifying the reasons for these gaps is crucial—without understanding the causes of deviation, neither the plan nor the performance can be improved.

8

The Litmus Test: Discipline and Consistency

Warrant Buffett has created tremendous wealth through a consistent compounding approach. In contrast, hedge fund managers who have generated extraordinary returns have, in many cases, accumulated significantly less wealth than Warrant Buffett.

Sir Warrant Buffett achieved an average annual return of 22 per cent over a span of seventy-plus years. In contrast, some hedge fund managers generate extraordinary returns of 66 per cent per annum—but only for a few years.

The key difference is that while hedge fund managers may deliver exceptionally high returns for short periods, Warrant Buffett consistently maintained his 22 per cent return for over seventy years.

This chapter is divided into the following sections:

- Without consistency, long-term goals cannot be accomplished.
- Avoid habits that negatively impact your journey.
- Not everything is worth doing—priorities must be clear (as discussed in Chapter 5).
- There will be ups and downs, but performance must remain consistent.

Without Consistency, Long-Term Goals Cannot Be Accomplished

M.S. Dhoni once said in an interview: '*Agar saal bhar mehnat ki hai to ek din se farak nahi padega, agar saal bhar mehnat nahi ki hai toh bhi ek din se farak nahi padega.*' (If you have worked hard all year, one day won't make a difference. If you haven't worked hard all year, one day still won't make a difference.)

Real-Life Example: The Power of Consistency and Sustainable Effort

Let's take a simple example of two individuals, Mr A and Mr B, who wanted to drive from location X to location Y, a distance of 1,000 km.

Mr A drove the first 300 km at an average speed to 120 km per hour. He was speeding, overtaking recklessly, and trying to drive as fast as possible. After completing the initial 300 km, he took a one-hour break before resuming his journey at the same average speed of 120 km per hour.

However, before completing the 300-km stretch, a traffic police officer fined him. As a result, Mr A wasted an hour dealing with the officer and then had to take another hour of rest.

During the final 400 km, the weather turned unfavourable. It suddenly started raining, and traffic conditions worsened due to heavy rainfall. Consequently, he could drive only at an average speed of 60 km per hour.

In summary, Mr A took fourteen hours and forty minutes to complete the 1,000-km journey from location X to location Y. Additionally, because he frequently exceeded the average speed limit, his fuel efficiency suffered—he consumed significantly more fuel than what is typically required for a 1,000-km journey.

On the other hand, Mr B maintained a more consistent approach. He followed all traffic rules and never exceeded the speed limit. The permitted speed on the road was 90 km per hour, and his average speed remained 80 km per hour. He took four breaks of thirty minutes each during the journey. As a result, Mr B reached location Y in fourteen hours and thirty minutes.

Key takeaways from the example:

- Overachieving your real capacity may be possible at times; however, it can lead to fatigue and require longer breaks to recover. We are not suggesting that you should never push your limits, but there is a difference between challenging yourself and exhausting all your energy.
- Consistent and steady effort often yields better outcomes. Mr B reached his destination in fourteen hours and thirty minutes, while Mr A, despite speeding, took fourteen hours and forty minutes.
- External factors beyond your control can affect your journey. In Mr A's case, unexpected rain and traffic jam impacted his travel time. Such situations can have an adverse effect on any long-term pursuit.
- Respecting laws and regulations is crucial. Otherwise, penalties and other consequences can be severe enough to nullify your entire effort. In some cases, they may prevent you from reaching your goal altogether.

For example, if you are building a business, a compliance with income tax and regulatory laws is essential. Similarly, your health and well-being should be a priority. In Mr A's case, excessive speeding could have resulted in an accident with severe consequences.

Whatever your goal, you must ensure that your health and well-being are not compromised in the long run. Of course, priorities must be set, and sacrifices may be necessary to achieve critical objectives. However, even if you fail in your mission, as long as you remain safe, you will always have another chance to succeed.

Avoid Habits That Negatively Impact Your Journey

Real-Life Example: Identifying and Elimination Habits that Hinder Progress

One day, Mr A looked in the mirror and realized that he was gaining weight. The next evening, while getting ready for a party, he noticed that his old clothes no longer fit him well. The following day, he decided that he needed to take action.

Mr A began researching online about ways to lose weight. He discovered that several factors are critical for maintaining a fit body, including exercise or workout, diet, and water intake.

Mr A was a corporate employee with a daily routine that involved long hours of sitting. He was not engaging in any physical exercise and was consuming excessive carbohydrates.

Understanding his habits and recognizing that he wanted a fit body rather than a muscular one, he decided that a daily workout might not be feasible. Instead, he focused on optimizing his diet and water intake.

After considering various factors, such as what he could carry for lunch at the office, he created a daily diet plan and followed it consistently. However, he made the following mistakes:

- Frequent parties: He attended parties once a week, where he consumed oily food and alcohol.
- Regular sweet consumption: He continued eating sugar and sweets frequently.
- Late-night snacking: He ate small portion of junk food (such as noodles and chips) late night on a daily basis.
- Excess calorie intake: In addition to consuming unhealthy food at parties and eating sweets, he often exceeded his daily calorie requirements.

After six months, when Mr A was not seeing any favourable outcomes, he realized that he might be making certain mistakes.

He decided to make the following changes to his lifestyle:

- He would completely quit sugar consumption, including sweets.
- He decided to attend only two parties in any one-month period. Apart from these occasions, he would entirely avoid oily food and alcohol.
- After having his dinner (at around 8 p.m.), he would not eat anything. If he could not control late-night hunger, he would eat only salads—that is, no carbohydrates and only easily digestible food.
- He would carefully monitor and control his portion sizes to avoid excess calorie intake.

With these small behavioural changes, the outcomes over the next six months were tremendous and clearly observable.

The key lesson from this example is that identifying incorrect habits or behaviours that negatively impact progress is essential.

To achieve better results, such habits must be consciously avoided. If an individual is aware of these detrimental behaviours but still does not eliminate them, it becomes nearly impossible to improve outcomes.

There Will Be Ups and Downs, but Performance Must Remain Consistent

Real-Life Example: The Importance of Perseverance through Difficult Times

Mr A started a restaurant. The business performed exceptionally well for the first six months. However, a global economic downturn caused a natural disaster (similar to COVID-19) that led to significant losses over the next six months. As a result, by the end of the first year, the restaurant's net earnings were negative.

As the economy began to recover, the initial reopening phase (the following six months) was not highly rewarding. Consumer behaviour had shifted—people were out less and travelling less frequently. Consequently, the restaurant operated at a break-even level or even at a loss for several months.

Adding to his struggles, Mr A lost a close family member who had been actively involved in the restaurant's operations.

After eighteen months, he decided to close the business. Ultimately, over this period, the restaurant yielded no net gain. He sold all the assets, along with the restaurant lease, to a buyer, Mr B, who was eager to continue running the business.

Mr B saw an opportunity to acquire an already operational restaurant at a discount. His vision was that the worst phase was over and that a strong resurgence in tourism and dining out was imminent.

Six months later, Mr A happened to pass by his former restaurant and saw that it was bustling with customers. Business appeared to be thriving again.

Feeling nostalgic, he decided to have a quick lunch. To his surprise, he noticed that most of the staff he had hired—from chefs to servers—were still there, with only a few having moved on. Even the menu remained unchanged.

He felt deeply regretful after that one meal.

Mr A had endured twelve months of adversity, but had he held on a little longer, the situation would have turned in his favour.

The business was recovering with the same team, the same menu, and the same operational structure. The only difference was that Mr B had weathered the tough times.

The key takeaway from the above example is that the path to achieving a challenging goal will always involve ups and downs. However, regardless of these fluctuations and difficult situations, it is essential to keep going and remain consistent.

9

Build your Skillset: Learn, Adapt, Improve

'The expert in anything was once a beginner.'

—Helen Hayes

This chapter is divided into the following sections:

- Learning, experience, and practise are essential for building the required skillset.
- Observe your mistakes or shortcomings and accept them.
- Address your mistakes or shortcomings and be ready for change.

Learning, Experience, and Practise Are Essential for Building the Required Skillset

To achieve a challenging goal, you must continuously improve yourself over time. Take the example of any successful personality—an entrepreneur, a cricketer, or anyone else—and compare them to when they first started their journey. There would undoubtedly be a clear and observable difference.

Those who consistently strive for self-improvement are the ones who ultimately reach their goals. Therefore, learning and continuous practise are essential for growth.

The objective should be to become the best and develop the necessary skillset to accomplish the goal.

Observe Your Mistakes or Shortcomings and Accept Them

'The first step toward change is awareness. The second step is acceptance.'

—Nathaniel Branden

Real-Life Example: Adapting Strategies and Strengthening Risk Management in Trading

We started derivative trading with a basic options strategy—covered puts—where we sold options on an underlying asset. Our intent was that if the spot price of the underlying asset fell below the strike price of the option contract, we would use our cash reserves to purchase the asset, effectively turning it into an investment.

This strategy proved highly profitable in the first year. However, in the second year, during a monthly expiry, several option contracts ended up in-the-money, requiring us to take delivery of multiple stocks in pre-decided lot sizes.

Since the covered put strategy had generated good profits initially, we neglected key risk management principles—we lacked sufficient funds to take delivery of the put options we had underwritten. As a result, we had no choice but to book a significant loss.

The very next day, the market surged, and the prices of most of the stocks we had bet on rose—many exceeding the strike price at which we had sold the options.

Key learnings from this experience:

- Market conditions are never constant. A strategy that worked efficiently in one year may fail in the next.
- Trading may seem simpler in profitable scenarios, but it involves much more, including risk management and position sizing.

At that point, we had two choices: quit trading, as we were still in net profit but lacked an alternative strategy, or continue with the same approach while implementing proper risk management and position sizing.

We chose the latter. In parallel, we decided to educate ourselves by reading trading books and watching learning videos. Over the next few months, we studied fundamental concepts such as price action, trend indicators, trading patterns, and trading strategies, including momentum trading, trend trading, and non-directional strategies.

Eventually, we adapted our approach—selling both call and put options based on indicators while maintaining strict position sizing. However, this new strategy led to another major loss due to the following mistakes:

- While we understood from books and videos that trading is speculation and risk management (especially stop-loss) is crucial, our lack of practical experience prevented us from respecting stop-loss levels. We always intended to cut losses but often hesitated, waiting for the price to return to the status-quo—a classic hope trade.
- By not adhering to stop-losses, we failed to respect our trading setup. The same indicators and patterns that previously signalled a 'buy' were now indicating a 'sell', leaving us uncertain about what to follow.

At this stage, quitting trading seemed like the obvious choice. Instead, we took a short break, reflected on our mistakes, and realized that while our trading principles were sound, our risk management had been weak.

When we resumed trading, we strictly adhered to stop-loss levels. This reduced our losses significantly, but we still struggled with maximizing profits. While we were cutting losses early, we were also booking profits too soon, leading to suboptimal overall performance.

We believed we had solved 50 per cent of the problem and needed to work on patience when booking profits.

Then came another challenge—factors beyond our control.

Gap-down opening after selling a put option: We had no control over the asset's opening price. Since the price opened significantly lower, we were not even given an opportunity to book the loss and respect the stop-loss.

We then thought that, given the price was already 10 per cent down from our stop-loss level, we should not book the loss at that point and should instead wait for it to recover (again, a hope trade).

The next day, the price dropped another 5 per cent (a total of 15 per cent below our stop-loss level).

A bigger problem arose because we had executed a stock option contract rather than an index option contract. As a result, volumes were very low, and spreads were substantially high.

At this point, even if we had decided to book the loss, we would have ended up paying significantly more than our actual loss.

Price surged after selling a put option: However, both of us were occupied with work and were unable to book the profit.

The next day, the asset's breakout failed, and our profit turned into a loss. At this stage, we were at a net loss in our overall trading journey.

The only logical decision now was to quit trading, as we were putting our hard-earned money at risk.

We then learned about trading bots (that is, algorithm-based trading machines or software) that involve minimal human intervention. The clear advantage of these bots is that they eliminate emotional biases in trading.

Trading decisions are made by computers based on pre-defined entry and exit principles. We also discovered that direction-based trading can be profitable. However, we lacked the complete infrastructure to leverage this strategy.

We began working on algorithmic trading, including back-testing our exiting trading strategies. We are currently using algo-trading platforms for direction-based trading.

Additionally, we manually execute non-directional trades (that is, deploying out-of-the-money call and put option for an underlying asset) with hedges on both sides. This ensures that even in the event of a black swan event, our losses do not exceed our overall earnings. These hedges are deployed at the time of executing the main trade.

Key takeaways from our journey:

- The only way to remain competitive in any journey is to keep learning and improving day by day through those learnings.

- There is no point in fighting against your mistakes. Shortcomings are inevitable, and it is important to identify them with an open mindset.
- Without recognizing your shortcomings, trying repeatedly without adjustment will only lead to frustration and failure.
- Negative outcomes will occur many times throughout the journey. However, every learning experience has a cost—treat losses or negative outcomes as the price of learning.
- Many circumstances or situations cannot be predicted at the start of the journey. They will become evident over time, and their solutions must be figured out along the way.

'We cannot solve our problems with the same thinking we used when we created them.'

—Albert Einstein

Address Your Mistakes or Shortcomings and Be Ready for Change

When working towards the accomplishment of a challenging goal, many aspects need to be learned over time. A rigid attitude can negatively impact outcomes. Therefore, be open to change—new ideas and corrective measures should be welcomed.

By embracing new ideas and addressing shortcomings, you will not only improve yourself but also strengthen your ability to compete effectively.

10

Ignore the Uncontrollable: Focus on What Matters

If you try to control everything and worry about things beyond your control, you are setting yourself up for a lifetime of frustration and misery.

This chapter is divided into the following sections:

- Differentiate between controllable and uncontrollable factors
- You cannot control your competitors—everyone is here to win
- Focus on what you can control, and don't overthink what you cannot
- Some events may adversely impact your journey, but those who persevere reach the finish line

Differentiate between Controllable and Uncontrollable Factors

In any difficult situation, there are two types of factors: those that can be controlled and those that cannot.

Real-Life Example: Focus on Controllable Factors while Adapting to Uncertainties

Mr A started a new business. In the journey of building a successful business, severable controllable factors came into play, including:

- Deciding on the business opportunity to pursue, such as identifying sectors with strong future potential (such as sectors where there is a gap between demand and supply, sectors prioritized by the government, or those attracting investor interest)
- Formulating business strategies, such as whether to pursue an acquisition or start afresh
- Hiring an investment banker to raise capital
- Reaching out to investors for funding
- Building a core management team

However, multiple factors remain beyond one's control, such as:

- Economic conditions
- The political environment
- Competitor's actions
- Tax and regulatory amendments introduced by the government and their potential impact—whether adverse or favourable—on the business

Mr A shortlisted various products for go-to-market evaluation and, based on market research analysis, decided to commence manufacturing glass panels used in solar cells (which retain energy).

This decision was largely influenced by a significant government push to promote clean and renewable sources of energy and to reduce dependence on non-renewable energy sources.

To support this shift, the government was offering a range of incentives for setting up manufacturing facilities, along with various discounts for end customers, to ensure adequate demand for solar cells.

Mr A recognized that the next fifteen years would likely witness a clear transformation in the energy sector.

However, Mr A was not alone in identifying this opportunity. Many large players had already entered the market, manufacturing similar products—an uncontrollable factor. He realized that innovation and cost-saving in the production process would be essential to remain competitive.

To this end, he hired bankers to raise capital and imported the best global technology for manufacturing glass panels. Additionally, he focused on building a strong research and development team to drive ongoing innovation and cost optimization.

Initially, Mr A faced difficulties securing contracts from clients across the country, as he had only one central manufacturing facility. He soon realized that a single, centralized facility was impractical for nationwide distribution. Within two years, he established four manufacturing units across different regions to better serve customers locally.

In the fourth year of operations, the government imposed anti-dumping duties on certain critical raw materials imported from neighbouring countries. Mr A responded by sourcing raw materials from other geographies, such as Europe and North America. Although these imports were slightly more expensive, he eventually began manufacturing these materials locally within his existing factories to reduce costs.

Furthermore, the government's tax holidays and incentives were only available for the initial eight to ten years. However, Mr A was already aware that the incentives were being offered only in the initial years to make the product financially attractive. In later years, these incentives might no longer be available. Mr A continued to focus on overseas markets, which were offering incentives for a similar shift, to drive growth.

Throughout his journey of building the business, Mr A concentrated on controllable factors and continually worked to improve them.

The key takeaway from the above example is that the best approach is to focus energy and resources on controllable aspects.

For uncontrollable factors, maintaining awareness—by reading newspaper, engaging in discussion, and staying informed—is beneficial, but direct influence is limited.

Be prepared to make necessary decisions or revisit existing ones to ensure your strategy remains adaptable and responsive to uncontrollable factors.

> *'Suffering arises from trying to control what is uncontrollable, or from neglecting what is within our power.'*
>
> —Epictetus

You Cannot Control Your Competitors—Everyone Is Here to Win

When working towards a challenging goal, we often try to understand what our competitors are doing. At times, we may attempt to influence their actions or strategize ways to reduce their chances of success.

It is important to remember that everyone is here to win, and everyone has the right to succeed—just as you do. Similarly, you also have the right to win and successfully achieve your challenging goal.

It is always beneficial to stay informed about what your competitors are doing. Such knowledge can help you identify areas for improvement by adopting better practices that they have implemented.

However, attempting to control your competitors' actions will not be beneficial in the long run. It is always better to focus your energy on achieving your own success rather than trying to undermine others.

> *'You can't control what the other athlete is going to do; you can't control anything except for your competition and how you execute the race or how you execute the task.'*
>
> —Michael Johnson

Focus on What You Can Control, and Don't Overthink What You Cannot

Instead of focusing on controllable aspects, we often tend to worry about things beyond our control. For example, a stock market trader might start wondering what would happen if a war broke out between two large nations—would the stock market crash?

As a trader, technical analysis (such as chart patterns or indicators) can help assess the potential direction of the market. However, unless there is a strong, clear trend, the probability of the market going up or down is often equal. In reality, no one can predict market movements with certainty or determine how high or low it will go.

Therefore, it is more effective to focus on strategy. If your technical analysis suggests a bullish outlook on a stock, your priority should not be predicting price movements but managing risks. You cannot control the stock's direction or price, but you can control your stop-loss—deciding in advance what action to take if the trade does not go as planned.

A similar approach should be applied when pursuing any challenging goal. You need to prepare for worst-case scenarios and be ready to adapt your decisions as circumstances change.

Overthinking potential situations beyond your control and trying to manage them is counterproductive. When you cannot control what is happening, challenge yourself to control how you respond—that is where your true power lies.

Some Events May Adversely Impact Your Journey, but Those Who Persevere Reach the Finish Line

There are times when an aspirant may lose all momentum and consider abandoning their journey. One such example is discussed below:

Real-Life Example: Loosing the Love of One's Life

Mr A had a strong ambition to become a naval officer. He successfully cleared the preliminary entrance exam, the mains exam, and the physical tests. He was preparing for the final interview round when, just before the scheduled date, he lost the love of his life—his girlfriend, whom he was planning to marry.

This event had a profound impact on Mr A. In an attempt to cope with the situation, he turned to drugs and alcohol.

Although he did attend the final interview, his performance was poor. The jury, in unanimous agreement, gave him a below-average rating. They were also surprised by the contrast between his earlier impressive performance in the preliminary and mains exams and his lacklustre showing during the interview.

The key message from this example is that if you have committed yourself to a particular goal and later face events that make you question that pursuit, do not give up. A few emotionally difficult moments can derail your entire journey and keep you from achieving your life's ambition.

11

Accept Reality: Work with It

'Acceptance doesn't mean resignation; it means understanding that something is what it is and that there's got to be a way through it.'

—Michael J. Fox

This discussion is divided into the following parts:

- Small advantages or benefits can sometimes make a big difference. You may not have all of them—but the truth remains unchanged, regardless of how difficult it is to accept.
- Outcomes are not always entirely dependent on your performance; other factors also play a role.

Small Advantages or Benefits Can Sometimes Make a Big Difference

Real-Life Example: Overcoming Disadvantages with Persistence and Hard Work

Many people who are born and brought up in small towns aspire to become actors or models. To pursue their dreams, they relocate from small towns to large cities. They join acting schools or modelling academies and work on both their physical appearance and performance skills.

However, despite attending numerous auditions, they are often unable to secure a debut role during the initial years. At the same time, some aspirants appear to be in a more advantageous position—often because their parents or grandparents were already part of the film industry.

By leveraging their industry connections, these aspirants were able to secure debut roles more easily. Additionally, they had the financial resources to invest in their debut if needed.

Moreover, when a debut movie features a family member of a successful film star (such as a parent or a grandparent), a certain level of marketing happens by default. This makes such projects more attractive to producers, increasing their willingness to invest.

The key point here is that competitors or fellow aspirants may have an upper hand in various aspects. However, from their perspective, why wouldn't they take advantage of an opportunity that was naturally available to them? Wouldn't you have done the same if you were in their position?

The simple reality is that when someone is not on the receiving end of an advantage, they may find it difficult to accept others enjoying similar benefits. However, the truth remains unchanged, regardless of our ability to accept it.

As we have discussed multiple times in this book, the only thing in your control as an aspirant is to keep giving your best and working hard. Do your best with whatever comes your way. God will be kind—have faith.

You can't control everything. Sometimes, you just need to relax and trust that things will work out.

You need to accept that certain advantages or benefits may be available to other aspirants. However, you must build your own strengths through hard work to achieve eventual success.

There are also many examples of successful personalities in the same industry who were not blessed with similar advantages but still secured a debut role after years of patience and perseverance.

Furthermore, a debut opportunity holds far greater significance for those who were not born into privilege compared to those who were. These individuals tend to have deep respect for their debut role, as they might have earned it after years of waiting and hard work. They are highly motivated to give their best effort, knowing that this one opportunity could shape their entire career.

Given their challenging journey, they understand that failing to capitalize on this debut role could make future opportunities even harder to come by. Since they may not have the means to create another entry point, they approach this moment with a 'now or never' mindset, determined to make the most of it.

Real-Life Example: Acknowledging Challenges and Focusing on Personal Effort

Whenever you prepare for a competitive exam, a certain level of reservation is allocated for specific categories of candidates. Often, individuals from the general category express frustration, saying that candidates benefitting from reservation score much lower yet still secure admission. Meanwhile, a general-category candidate, despite scoring higher than those in the reserved category, may not gain admission.

However, it is important to recognize that reservation applies to all candidates. It is not a system designed to impact only you negatively. Moreover, there is significant competition within the reserved category itself. Only the most deserving candidates within that category secure admission.

There are reasons why reservation exits, and when you choose to pursue a challenging goal, you are already aware of such factors.

So, when making a decision about a challenging goal, it is important to understand potential obstacles—such as reservation, nepotism, etc.—and fully accept them.

Once you are aware of these challenges and still choose to pursue your goal, there is no point in feeling disheartened by them along the way, especially when faced with setbacks.

'I accept reality and dare not question it.'

—Walt Whitman

Outcomes Are Not Always Entirely Dependent on Your Performance

Real-Life Example: Navigating Workplace Favouritism

Similar to the situations discussed earlier, in corporate environments, we sometimes feel that we are not treated equally compared to others.

For instance, consider Mr A, who works at a large MNC. He is a high performer and has exceeded his business targets. However, when it comes to promotions, salary increments, or securing the best opportunities, his boss prefers other candidates on the team.

At times, we may feel that we are not treated fairly, but this perception may not always reflect the full reality. Favouritism often exists in workplaces for various reasons. For example, a preferred candidate might have worked with the boss for ten–fifteen years, developing a strong personal rapport and earning a sense of loyalty.

In such cases, there is little one can do to change these dynamics. These are harsh realities that must be accepted. No matter where we go, such factors will continue to exist in one form or another.

> *'Favouritism manifests itself in all departments of government, public and private. It is harder to avoid because it is so natural.'*
>
> —Thomas Chandler Haliburton

The key takeaway from the above example is that multiple factors determine the outcome, including some that are beyond the aspirant's control and may, at times, negatively affect the result (for example, favouritism).

In the short term, outcomes may not be entirely dependent on the amount of effort put in by the aspirant. However, it is important for the aspirant to accept this reality and continue doing what is right—including the practices discussed in this book.

In the long term, the outcomes are likely to be more favourable.

12

Forecasting and Assumptions: Limits of Prediction

'There are many talented people who haven't fulfilled their dreams because they overthought it, or they were too cautious and unwilling to take a leap of faith.'

—James Cameron

This discussion is divided into the following parts:

- When pursuing unprecedented goals, outcomes cannot be precisely computed—forecasting may not be the right approach; a leap of faith is the only way
- Forecasting relies on assumptions—predictions and actual results may differ

When Pursuing Unprecedented Goals, Outcomes Cannot Be Computed

Let us consider a real-life example to understand that, when pursuing unprecedented goals, an aspirant cannot truly predict or calculate the outcome.

Real-Life Examples: Writing This Book—Embracing Uncertainty and Taking a Leap of Faith

When we were writing this book—our first, and one we believe to be a challenging goal—a common question kept coming to mind: if this book is published by a reputed publisher, how much would we earn from it? The truth is that no one can predict the outcome in numerical terms.

Since this is our first book, we are debut writers with no prior experience or historical record. How, then, can anyone accurately predict the outcome?

We can make assumptions and try to forecast various scenarios—will this book become a bestseller? Will it sell enough copies to meet our worst-case expectations? But how do we truly know?

A more meaningful approach would be to ensure that our efforts are not driven by speculative predictions of probable outcomes—especially when those outcomes are highly uncertain.

We chose this goal after careful evaluation (as discussed in earlier chapters) and for our own reasons. Therefore, let us not attempt to compute the outcome.

The purpose of discussing the above example is to highlight that forecasting cannot provide definitive answers when it comes to decisions about pursuing unprecedented or challenging goals.

In the case of new ideas or businesses, a founder can never predict the outcomes with certainty. No one knows how far a new idea or business will go or what impact it will create—though a certain degree of analysis based on assumptions is always possible.

However, much depends on execution, external factors, and dynamic circumstances. Therefore, the only reasonable approach in such cases is to take a leap of faith—and just do it.

Forecasting Relies on Assumptions—Predictions and Actual Results May Differ

> *'All depends really on what kinds of assumptions you make. When you're forecasting things that will be happening 50 to 100 years in the future, it's really hard to predict what's going to happen that far out, so you have to make a bunch of assumptions.'*
>
> —Richard Harris

As we discussed earlier, if we take the example of any successful founder and look back in history, they never truly knew whether their business would grow big or successful.

Everything that is big today started as something very small at some point in time.

Apple (1976–80)

Amazon (1994–2009)

Images showing the first office locations of Apple and Amazon.

Source: https://www.wikipedia.org

At some stage, every founder must take a risk—a leap of faith.

While data analysis (both historical and projected) has its benefits—it aids decision-making and helps formulate strategies—it may not be wise to rely on forecasting to predict outcomes.

When starting something new, there is no definitive way to determine how far the journey will go.

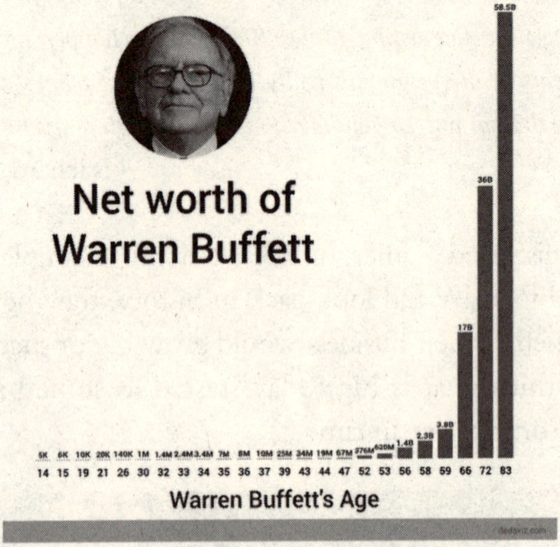

Diagram showing the rise in net worth of Sir Warren Buffet in comparison to his age.
Source: https://www.marketwatch.com/

The above diagram shows that it took around thirty years to reach the $1 million mark and a further twenty-six years to reach the $1 billion mark.

Additionally, the period from the age of fifty-six to the present has been tremendously rewarding.

The key point here is that at the age of fourteen, reaching a net worth of $58.5 billion would have seemed impossible, given that his actual wealth at the time was just $5,000. Furthermore, through his journey, Sir Warren Buffett likely had no idea that he would eventually amass such a vast fortune.

13

Luck and Destiny: The Unpredictable Factor

'Luck is very important. Of course, you can't wait for luck because it won't come while you start a journey. Luck may eventually come to you.'

—Jack Ma

We will divide this discussion into the following parts:

- Sometimes, everything is perfect, but luck is not in your favour
- Better luck next time—Restart
- If you succeed, always remember that luck was in your favour
- Similar efforts may lead to different outcomes due to certain decisions
- There may be something better for you—destiny cannot be changed

Sometimes, Everything Is Perfect, but Luck Is Not in Your Favour

Many times, everything seems perfect—the aspirant has done everything required to achieve the goal—yet luck does not appear to be in their favour.

There is no definitive answer as to why luck eludes some people or why such setbacks occur.

Let us consider a few examples to understand the role of luck in the journey.

Example from the Movie M.S. Dhoni: The Untold Story

Mahi (M.S. Dhoni) was selected for the Ranji Trophy. A day before his departure, he was informed that he needed to reach Kolkata the next morning.

However, his draft admission letter for the Ranji Trophy was delayed in transit. His friends pooled their savings and arranged a vehicle for overnight travel to Kolkata. They all travelled through the night from Ranchi to Kolkata.

Unfortunately, they arrived at Kolkata airport slightly late, causing Mahi to miss his hard-earned opportunity to play in the Ranji Trophy.

Real-Life Examples: The Risks of Skipping the Unfamiliar

In competitive exams, candidates prepare thoroughly. However, they sometimes skip certain topics or chapters, assuming they are not very relevant or simply because they find them uninteresting.

From my own experiences in the CA final exams, I have seen that questions from such topics or chapters were sometimes included as compulsory questions and carried significant weight. Not attempting those questions can greatly impact the final outcome.

Real-Life Examples: When Uncontrollable Factors Disrupt Well-Laid Plans

When I was a manager in an MNC, I (Anuj) was keen to move to a developed or mature market for better opportunities. I was actively looking for a shift to a developed city, such as London or Dubai.

After months of hard work and multiple interviews, I was on the verge of receiving a job offer from the London office of my organization.

By late January 2020, the placement team had provided informal confirmation via email that they would roll out the offer within couple of weeks, while the visa process would be initiated simultaneously.

However, in February 2020, news reports began surfacing about a virus wreaking havoc in China. Soon after, the world went under lockdown.

The placement team from the London office informed me that all overseas hiring processes had been put on hold, and they would need to reassess their hiring strategy.

It was possible that, for the foreseeable future, foreign candidates would not be considered. Additionally, overall hiring decisions were being re-evaluated due to the uncertainty surrounding business operations in the wake of such an unprecedented event.

As discussed earlier, there is no definitive answer as to why luck does not favour someone or why such things happen.

One should not spend time and energy trying to identify the reasons behind bad luck. Sometimes, it simply isn't your day, or in a competitive scenario, someone else may be better prepared then you at that one crucial moment.

Instead, when outcomes are unfavourable due to bad luck, the strategy discussed in the subsequent section can be adopted.

Better Luck Next Time—Restart

If you believe you have done everything necessary to achieve your goal but were held back by bad luck, say, an unfortunate day, or a minor shortcoming, you need to restart.

As we have discussed multiple times in this book, it is unjustified to change your goal simply because you have encountered your first setback.

ICC World Cup 2023: The India Story

India dominated the tournament, winning all nine group-stage matches, including a victory over Australia, and then defeating New Zealand in the semi-final to reach the final.

However, in the World Cup final, the Aussies bowled India out for a below-par total of 240 on a tricky pitch. They then chased it down in 43 overs, securing a six-wicket win and claiming the world title.

Rohit Sharma reflected on the loss, saying, 'The result hasn't gone our way, and we know that we were not good enough on the day.'

Sometimes, it simply isn't your day, or someone else is better prepared then you at that one crucial moment.

The outcome is what it is; historically, there is nothing that can be changed.

Therefore, you need to accept the unfavourable outcome with a pinch of salt and gather the strength to restart, so that you can transform into a better version of yourself for the next opportunity.

If You Succeed, Always Remember that Luck Was in Your Favour

Sometimes, luck is on your side, and you are rewarded for it.

Let's discuss a few examples.

Real-Life Example: Seizing Opportunities Created by Unexpected Changes

Mr A was due for a promotion to a leadership role as group CFO in an MNC. However, the company already had a long-serving group CFO who was performing exceptionally well. Since there was no other leadership role available for him, the chances of Mr A being promoted within the organization were slim.

Unexpectedly, the existing group CFO decided to leave the company after being offered the role of group CEO (president) at a large organization. He saw this as a better opportunity, as it would give him a broader strategic role. The management attempted to retain him by offering better incentives and rewards, but he ultimately decided to move on.

As a result of his departure, a vacancy for group CFO was created. To fill this position, Mr A was immediately promoted to group CFO.

Real-Life Example: When Luck Overrides Preparation in Short-Term Success

Mr A was preparing for an entrance exam, which followed a multiple-choice format. Due to a shortage of time, he studied for only six hours one day before the exam.

Instead of solving problems to assess his competency, he randomly reviewed past exam questions and mock test papers. During his preparation, most of the answers he guessed on his own were incorrect. However, he also checked the correct answers to validate his estimates.

By sheer luck, the majority of the questions in the actual exam were the same as those he had reviewed during his six-hour preparation. Since he remembered many of the answers, he managed to score passing marks.

The key takeaway from both of the above examples is that there is always an element of luck in any journey.

You can only focus on your hard work, skillset, and efforts. Luck must play its own role.

If the ultimate outcome is favourable, it is a combination of various factors, along with luck, that results in success.

It is not purely our hard work, skillset, and efforts that lead to a favourable outcome. So, whenever you succeed, remember that the Almighty was kind to you and that luck was in your favour.

Similar Efforts May Lead to Different Outcomes Due to Certain Decisions

Real-Life Example: The Impact of Investment Timing and Decision-Making

Mr A and Mr B both invested Rs 5 lakh each in a stock (symbol: XYZ). During the first year, the stock delivered a 10 per cent return. However, Mr B needed money for a personal emergency, so he sold his shares. In the following year, the overall market underperformed, and XYZ delivered a negative return of 15 per cent.

By the end of second year, Mr A was at a net loss on the invested capital, and Mr B, having used the money for a year and avoiding losses, was content.

At this point, Mr B reinvested Rs 5 lakh in XYZ. In the third year, XYZ showed no net gain. Both Mr A and Mr B saw no returns over a three-year period.

At the end of third year:

- Mr B exited XYZ and reinvested the entire amount in PQR, the second-largest company and a top-performing stock over a ten-year period.
- Mr A remained invested in XYZ, convinced it was the best stock among the top fifty, despite analysts releasing bearish reports on it. Mr A believed it was only a matter of time before XYZ rebounded, and when it did, investors would buy it at a much higher price.

In the fourth year:

- PQR performed poorly, delivering a negative return of 15 per cent.
- XYZ surged, making up for four years of underperformance with a 75 per cent return in a single year.

Analysts, who were once bearish on XYZ, turned highly bullish. Seeing this, Mr B exited his investment in PQR at a 15 per cent and reinvested in XYZ at the beginning of the fifth year. However, after a strong 75 per cent rally, profit booking led to a 5 per cent negative return for XYZ in the fifth year.

At the end of five years:

- Mr A stood at a net profit, exceeding the risk-free return and his expected IRR.

- Mr B, despite investing in the same stock for most of the period, was at a net loss.

Certain decisions made by Mr B adversely impacted his overall outcome.

The key point here is that the strategic decisions you make at different phases of your journey have a strong impact on the outcome.

As discussed earlier, the ultimate outcome or result is a combination of various factors. Hence, there is no point comparing your outcomes with those of other aspirants, even if your efforts may have been similar.

Similar efforts can lead to different outcomes, primarily due to different decisions made by you and other aspirants at various stages of your journey.

There May Be Something Better for You—Destiny Cannot Be Changed

If you have done everything possible from your side and made the necessary attempts to succeed, then accept whatever has happened as the will of God and move on.

> *'We cannot change our destiny; we just have to have the courage to know what it is and accept it.'*
>
> —Cinderpelt

14

Overcome Obstacles: Keep Moving Forward

'If you focus on the goal, you will overcome all obstacles. If you focus on the obstacles, you will never reach your goal.'

—Mukesh Ambani

We will divide this chapter into the following sections:

- Obstacles exist in everything we do—stretch beyond limits
- Visualize your goal to boost motivation
- Identify the obstacles standing between you and your goal, then find a way around them
- Obstacles make you tougher—keep facing them

Obstacles Exist in Everything We Do—Stretch beyond Limits

Real-Life Example: The Power of Vision and Overcoming Fear of Obstacles

Mr A, Mr B, and Mr C were three young friends. One day, they were discussing their future aspirations. Mr A said he wanted to become a doctor. However, Mr B responded by pointing out the challenges: Mr A would have to study hard for years. Even after all that effort, a doctor's job is difficult—long operation hours, sudden emergencies at odd times, and the emotional difficulty of dealing with blood and organs.

Despite this, Mr A was confident. He replied, 'I see myself as the best heart specialist in this country someday.' He continued, 'My vision is clear—whenever someone faces a heart-related problem, the first name that should come to mind is Dr A.' Mr A could vividly visualize his goal.

Now, Mr C shared his aspiration—he wanted to become an entrepreneur and build a global business. Once again, Mr B reacted with scepticism. He pointed out that similar businesses have a low success rate, and raising capital would be difficult since investors fund only a handful of startups.

In response, Mr C confidently stated that he would start a global coffee chain using a franchise model. To help his friends visualize his goal, Mr C gave them a scenario: 'Imagine I'm travelling to Spain and meeting an old college batchmate after a long time. My friend suggests meeting at a coffee store—one that happens to be a franchise of my coffee brand. As we sit there, my friend tells me that this is the best coffee shop in the country and that people love the entire experience. Then, I surprise him by saying that this global coffee brand is mine.'

Years passed. While Mr A and Mr C pursued their dreams, Mr B remained focused on obstacles rather than possibilities. He accomplished little in life.

Thirty years later, the three friends planned a reunion. At the reunion, Mr B asked Mr A and Mr C how their lives were going.

Mr A, now one of the country's top heart specialists, and Mr C, a leading business tycoon, had hectic and challenging lives. However, they were both deeply fulfilled. They talked about their daily schedules, their teams, their family time, recent vacations, and how much they loved what they were doing.

When it was Mr B's turn to share, he revealed that he ran a small grocery store in his town. For an hour, he complained about the struggles he faced: no holidays, early morning openings and late-night closings, difficulty in finding reliable workers, low profit margins, and heavy competition in the area.

While Mr A and Mr C had embraced challenges and turned their visions into reality, Mr B had remained stuck in his fear of obstacles, never moving forward.

Key takeaways from the example, specifically in relation to challenging goals, are as follows:

- No matter what challenging goal you choose, there will always be obstacles along the way. The journey will not be a cakewalk.
- Every individual has the choice to focus on the path that works best for them after carefully evaluating both the good and bad aspects.
- If no option seems right for you, it may be better to avoid pursuing challenging goals altogether.
- By focusing on your goal and visualizing your destination, you will find motivation to overcome obstacles—making the journey seem easier and more rewarding.

Visualize Your Goal to Boost Motivation

If you have a true passion and love for your goal, imagining the destination will ease your troubles and give you the strength to overcome obstacles.

Real-Life Example: Focusing on the Destination Rather than the Obstacles

Mr A and Mr B planned a trip from New Delhi to Goa. However, they were making travel arrangements at the last moment—the trip was scheduled for the following week.

Mr A suggested taking a flight. Mr B immediately objected saying flights would be expensive. Mr A then proposed travelling by train. However, when Mr B checked availability, he found that no direct trains were available.

Mr A suggested driving from New Delhi to Goa, pointing out that he had a full-time driver who was willing to handle the long journey. Once again, Mr B was hesitant, arguing that such a long drive would be uncomfortable.

Despite having two small children, Mr A was still enthusiastic about the road trip. He reasoned that with a luxury car and a driver, the journey would be manageable. Mr B, however, focused on the difficulties—traffic, finding places to stop for meals, and the exhaustion of a long drive.

At this point, Mr A reminded him: 'Focus on the Goa trip. Once we reach Goa, we can relax, party, and explore places conveniently with our own car.' But Mr B remained fixed on the obstacles instead of the end goal.

The key point here is that it is important to focus on the obstacles in order to find ways to deal with them. However, focusing solely on the obstacles will not lead you to your destination.

In every option you may choose to reach your goal, there will be some obstacle or another. However, you need to choose a path and deal with the obstacles that arise along the way.

If you focus only on the obstacles (as Mr B did), you will lack the strength to overcome them, and the excitement to reach your ultimate destination will be lost.

Identify the Obstacles Standing between You and Your Goal, Then Find a Way Around

Someone once said, 'You could walk on water; you only need to know where the stones are placed.'

No one is born with a natural ability to withstand challenges. Resilience is something you develop throughout life.

And never expect everything to come to you on a silver platter—that only happens in the grave. As long as you are alive, you will have to overcome obstacles and surmount difficulties.

Analyse your obstacles and find a way around them.

Obstacles Make You Tougher—Keep Facing Them

Real-Life Example: Building Strength and Resilience through Progressive Challenges

Mr A goes to the gym daily. During the first six months, he lifted 5 kg to 10 kg weights for muscle-building exercises. Over the next six months, he increased his lifting capacity to 15 kg to 20 kg. However, in the initial days after this transition, lifting the heavier weight was extremely difficult for him.

By his third year, he was consistently lifting 35 kg to 40 kg for all exercises. Now, lifting 25 kg feels like the easiest task for him. His exposure to increasing challenges helped him build resilience. By tackling progressively tougher obstacles, he found that simpler challenges became much easier.

Obstacles play a crucial role in our lives—they make us stronger and help us develop the resilience needed to overcome even greater difficulties.

15

Use Comparison Wisely: For Growth, Not Doubt

'Comparison is the thief of joy.'

—Theodore Roosevelt

This chapter is divided into the following sections:

- There will always be someone prettier, smarter, or younger
- Everyone has their own strengths and weaknesses
- Beginners should not compare the outcomes of their efforts with those of industry or domain leaders
- Comparison can be useful for identifying best practices and incorporating them into your own journey

There Will Always Be Someone Prettier, Smarter, or Younger

Real-Life Example: Focusing on Self-Improvement Instead of Comparing with Others

Miss Ruby wanted to become a model. She enrolled in a beauty contest, which received 10,000 applications. A total of twenty candidates were shortlisted, and fortunately, she was one of them.

She was invited to stay at a top-class resort for fifteen days to compete alongside the other selected candidates. She was overjoyed to have made it to the competition.

One the very first day, she met the other nineteen shortlisted candidates over dinner. After dinner, she returned to her room and spent the next three hours thinking about them. These thoughts ran through her mind:

- Alpa is so beautiful; it is impossible to defeat her in this beauty contest.
- Nicky looks stunning—no one could beat her.
- Stacy has an incredible dressing sense; she was the best-dressed at dinner.
- Bharti is great at expressing herself, and her communication skills are outstanding. She connects well with people and would be able to answer any question from the panel with confidence. The panel will definitely select her.

For those three hours, she never once considered why she was among the twenty candidates chosen out of 10,000 applications.

The key takeaway is that while others may be better than you in certain aspects, your focus should always be on yourself, not on them.

It is valuable to recognize how others excel, as this can inspire you to challenge yourself and improve. However, there is no benefit in feeling demotivated by their strengths.

Whenever you compete for a challenging goal, you will encounter candidates who may surpass you in many ways. Yet, what truly matters is overcoming your shortcomings, persevering, and staying committed to the challenge—because that is how you ultimately succeed.

Everyone Has Their Own Strengths and Weaknesses

Real-Life Example: Recognizing Individual Strengths and Their Role in Team Success

Consider a cricket team, Hurricane Royales. The playing eleven consists of four batsmen, four bowlers, two all-rounders, and one wicketkeeper-batsman.

Among the four batsmen, two players—Mr A and Mr B—are openers. Although both have experience playing in the middle order, they do not perform well in that position. They prefer playing an innings with a new ball.

Whenever the team wins the toss and chooses to bat first, Mr A and Mr B have the potential to play the first 20 overs and score 100+ runs together. Mr A is an aggressive batsman, scoring quickly with boundaries, while Mr B plays a more calculated and steady innings, supporting Mr A. Mr A puts pressure on the opposition, whereas Mr B focuses on rotating the strike.

If either of them gets out, Mr C or Mr D step in as a replacement, depending on the situation. Mr C is an aggressive player and would replace Mr A, while Mr D who plays similarly to Mr B, would take his place. This strategic coordination works well for the team.

One day, the opening order was changed. Instead of Mr A and Mr B, Mr A and Mr C were set to open. As expected, both started smashing the bowlers, scoring a quick 50 runs in just 3 overs. However, they got out in quick succession.

Mr B and Mr D then came in at the next batting order. Staying true to their natural playing styles, they took a cautious and calculated approach. The game seemed slow, but they were aware that the batsmen following them were either all-rounders or bowlers. They played for the next 30 overs, managing to take the total to just 150 runs.

By the end of 50 overs, the team had scored 220 runs—a modest total. Now, the bowlers had a crucial role to play, as the batting lineup had not performed exceptionally well.

The team had two fast pacers and two spinners. The pacers struck early, bringing the match to an even playing field. The spinners then ensured that runs were not given away easily, maintaining the run-rate and making strike rotation difficult for the other team. Additionally, the wicketkeeper played a crucial role by securing two runouts.

If someone scores quick runs, he may be taking unwarranted risks. However, sometimes that approach is necessary, while at other times, it may not be the best strategy. Similarly, if someone plays a slow and steady innings, it may be crucial when early wickets have fallen, but it does not always contribute to a high total. In summary, every player contributed in some way to the team's victory.

The purpose of this example is to highlight that everyone has their own strengths and weaknesses, which set them apart from others. These differentiators can have both positive and negative aspects. Every strength has its own value, and there is no need to compare one person's strengths with another's.

Beginners Should Not Compare the Outcomes of Their Efforts with Those of Industry or Domain Leaders

Real-Life Example: The Power of Brand Value and Long-Term Trust

Mr A started a new restaurant, Cheetah. He hired a staff of ten, including chefs, servers, and helpers. He also paid freelancers to perform live music at his restaurant on weekend evenings.

The prices of all food items were very reasonable. Additionally, the restaurant offered up to 30 per cent discounts (on already reasonable prices) for customers who purchased subscriptions or reserved tables through mobile apps.

The staff was very friendly, the portion sizes were generous, and the food was well presented. The menu featured signature dishes and cocktails, which received excellent reviews. Customers often returned to order these special items.

However, the restaurant's rent was very high, as the space was leased in a prime location. Despite strong ratings and positive feedback, the restaurant was operated at an average occupancy of only 50 per cent.

Cheetah remained open for over twelve hours a day and was typically the last food outlet to close in the entire market. If someone was looking for food at midnight, Cheetah was one of the few places still serving customers.

Even with all these efforts, the restaurant struggled financially and ultimately operated at a net loss.

Good things take time!

On the other hand, there was a famous restaurant in the same market, located just near Cheetah. This restaurant, named Babar, had been operating for the past thirty years.

Babar was well known and highly reputed. It was also very expensive. There were no discounts—on the contrary, multiple service charges applied.

A one-day prior reservation was mandatory. Yes, you had to book a table at least a day in advance to dine at Babar for either lunch or dinner.

Additionally, Babar was open for only five hours a day—two and a half hours during lunch and another two and a half hours for dinner.

While the pricing was high, the restaurant offered a great ambience, and the food was good, though arguably not worth the price. This was not a restaurant for everyone.

Even with these conditions, Babar maintained a 90 per cent occupancy rate. The remaining 10 per cent non-occupancy was due to last-minute reservation cancellations.

Despite its high process and limited hours, Babar was a highly profitable restaurant.

The key difference here is brand value and trust, which Babar has built over the years. Babar is a go-to restaurant for many people. Customer feedback consistently states that Babar never disappoints and remains their preferred dining destination.

There is no point in comparing these two restaurants. Brand value and trust takes time to develop—it happens over the years. If you are just starting a business, don't feel discouraged by comparing yourself to those who are already successful in the industry.

Those who are successful today once started from the same place where you are now. They represent the present and have earned the right to reap the rewards of their years of hard work.

You are here to create the future. So, focus on investing, keep working hard, and trust that returns will come over time.

Comparison Can Be Useful for Identifying Best Practices and Incorporating Them into Your Own Journey

Real-Life Example: Embracing Effective Study Practices for Better Outcomes

Mr A and Mr B were good friends, both preparing for a competitive exam. They attended tuition classes together.

Mr B never took summary notes during the lessons and did not attempt problems during the problem-solving breaks provided by the tutor. However, Mr A made summary notes during class and actively solved problems during the allocated break time.

One day, after a month of attending tuition classes, Mr B asked from Mr A, 'Is there any benefit in making summary notes and solving problems during class? All this content is already available in the book. The tuition class is mainly for understanding that content.'

Mr A responded that while he would read books for detailed study, he would need summary notes for revision before the exam. Having concise notes would help him quickly review the entire subject a day before the test.

Mr B agreed, realizing that it would be impossible to go through a 700-page book in a single day, making summary notes essential. Then, he asked Mr A why he solved problems in class when detailed solutions were already available in the book.

Mr A explained that whenever he solved a question in tuition, he used a stopwatch to check whether he could complete it within the allocated time—mimicking an exam environment. He noted that this classroom setting was similar to an exam hall, something he might not replicate at home. Besides, he could always use the book for additional practice.

Mr B realized that both practices were highly effective and decided to incorporate them into his own preparation.

The key takeaway from this example is the importance of being open to identifying better practices and adopting them when necessary. If something is helpful, why not use it? There is no harm in adopting good practices.

16

Not Everyone Succeeds: The Climb Gets Tougher

We have divided this discussion into the following parts:

- Not everyone reaches the top
- The journey becomes harder—only the tough prevails
- Certain events may negatively impact your progress. The one who perseveres till the end reaches the final goal

Not Everyone Reaches the Top

Difficulties keep increasing as we move forward. In the initial phases, growth may be easy; however, it becomes more challenging as we progress.

Example 1: The Increasing Challenges of Competition

Let's take the example of Master Chintan (aged fifteen). He dreamed of representing his country in cricket (that is, becoming part of the international cricket team). He joined a reputed cricket academy in his town. Many participants in the academy played cricket as a hobby, while a few pursued it for passion and fitness. Even fewer aimed to eventually join the international cricket team.

Chintan played cricket for three years (until the age of eighteen) and was selected for his academy's dream team, which competed against other similar academies in the town. He was a wicketkeeper-batsman. It was his first tournament at that scale, where he competed against the best players from each academy. His performance throughout the tournament was average (scoring an average of 30 runs per match). He did not receive any accolades or awards during the tournament.

A year later, at nineteen, another city-level tournament was announced. This time, Chintan was better prepared to excel. He was awarded the Best Wicketkeeper of the Tournament and also scored the highest runs among all participants, earning the Player of the Tournament award.

Due to his outstanding performance, he became eligible to apply for the state-level team. However, he was one of 120 players eligible for selection, making the competition significantly tougher. His previous accolades (Best Wicketkeeper and Player of the Tournament) earned him bonus points and a chance for direct entry into the state team, provided he cleared the entrance match.

For the entrance match, there were ten teams of twelve players each. Chintan was part of the Royal Challengers. The selection criteria required that, regardless of whether his team won, he needed to score at least 50 runs and outperform all other wicketkeepers in terms of runs scored. He played a crucial innings of 55 runs, and fortunately, his team won the match. However, despite his team's victory, some of his teammates did not make it to the final state team. Players from other teams with similar credentials and bonus points were selected based on their individual performances.

Once the state team was selected, the competition shifted to playing against other state-level teams, each comprising the best players from their respective states.

For the next four years, Chintan continued playing state-level cricket, participating in tournaments against other state teams. However, his initial performance at this level was not remarkable. While he frequently scored over 100 runs in city-level academy matches, he failed to reach that milestone in any state-level tournament for an entire year.

One day, his city-level cricket academy organized a charity match and invited him to participate. During this match, he scored 120 runs and stumped two players behind the wicket.

A key reason for his strong performance was that no other state-level players were participating—his opponents were from the same city-level academy. Chintan realized that while his skill level had remained consistent (that is, it had not deteriorated), the level of competition in state-level tournaments had increased significantly. State-level players were far more competitive than those in city-level cricket academies. These highly skilled opponents, with their superior bowling attacks, made it increasingly difficult for him to score runs.

This experience taught him an important lesson: the challenges would only continue to intensify. Only the best players across state teams would earn the opportunity to play for the national cricket team.

Key conclusions from the example are as follows:

- Difficulties keep increasing as we progress in our journey

- Growth is easier in the initial phase
- As we advance, competition becomes tougher

In the early stages, you may have successful precedents to leverage. However, beyond a certain point, you may need to forge your own path. Additionally, while the number of competitors may decrease, however, their competency will be significantly higher.

Example 2: Overcoming Business Growth Challenges
Mr A wanted to start a solar cell manufacturing company. These cells serve as raw materials for the production of solar panels, which are used to generate solar energy. He was motivated to enter this business due to the increasing push—both from the government and the private sector—towards renewable and clean energy, reducing reliance on conventional energy sources.

The idea sounded appealing to Mr A. He raised the necessary capital from friends and family. Meanwhile, he was doing research on other companies who have already started solar cell manufacturing.

Based on his research, he was able to make key decisions regarding the business setup, including selecting a feasible location for the manufacturing plant, estimating per-unit production costs, setting the sale price, and calculating unit-level profit.

He also obtained annual reports of established players who had entered the industry five to seven years earlier. Since much of the essential initial data was publicly available, he leveraged this information and successfully launched his manufacturing operations.

Mr A was adept at identifying solutions to various business challenges. He built strong connections with large solar panel manufacturers. Within the next three years, the business began to thrive.

By the fifth year since incorporation, the company had reached a significant milestone, achieving a production scale comparable to the companies he had originally studied during his initial research. In terms of annual output and the number of manufacturing plants, his business was now on par with those established players.

However, the next phase of growth was far more challenging, with no clear precedents to follow. For nearly a year, there were no new ideas or innovations, and the business operated in auto-pilot mode. It is important to note that when Mr A started the company, there was a gap between demand and supply, which he successfully leveraged for growth.

However, over time, many new players entered the market. By the end of the sixth year, the demand-supply gap had significantly narrowed, limiting further expansion through traditional means.

Recognizing this, Mr A devised a new growth strategy. He began acquiring companies in overseas markets to manufacture solar cells and sell the output locally. The local companies benefited from government incentives, tax rebates, and other advantages. Meanwhile, his Indian competitors remained focused on domestic manufacturing and exports.

In the seventh year, Mr A successfully completed three acquisitions in different countries. To manage customer relationships, he set up local business development teams in each of these markets.

Over the next three years, (up to the completion of the tenth year since incorporation), Mr A continued expanding into new jurisdictions, either by setting up new manufacturing units or acquiring domestic manufacturing companies.

Throughout this period, he faced numerous challenges, including competition from local players and restrictions on further capital investment. Despite these challenges, his strategic approach enabled his company to capture approximately 30 per cent of the market share, making it the second-largest player in the industry. The largest player held a 50 per cent market share, while the remaining 20 per cent was distributed among multiple unorganized players.

The only real competitor was the company that held a 50 per cent market share. The market leader had developed its technology through in-house R&D, which was patented. This proprietary technology allowed them to manufacture at a lower cost, resulting in due better profit margins. Additionally, they had the capability to reduce market prices and regain lost market share if necessary.

Mr A had achieved a 30 per cent market share through strategic decisions and the competency of his management team. However, his company's manufacturing process was not unique, and existing capabilities were not sufficient to drive further growth.

To address this, Mr A hired a team of researchers and gave them a mandate: develop the smallest possible solar cell with the highest possible energy storage capacity.

Over the next three years, the team successfully created the smallest solar cell available in the market, capable of storing 10 times more energy than conventional cells. However, the manufacturing cost was slightly higher.

Despite this breakthrough, the company was unable to significantly increase its market share. The new cells found strong demand in the automobile industry, but they failed to attract customers for other applications. Recognizing this limitation, Mr A instructed the team to explore ways to reduce manufacturing costs.

Their global presence proved to be an advantage in solving this challenge. The raw material used to produce the new solar cells was available in certain overseas locations at 50 per cent lower cost. By sourcing raw materials from these locations, the company significantly reduced production expenses.

Over the years, this cost optimization—combined with the new technology—allowed the company to expand its market share to 65 per cent, surpassing the former marker leader.

Key conclusions from the above example:

- Challenges continued to increase as Mr A expanded his market share.
- In the initial phase, setting up the manufacturing plant was relatively easy since most of the required information was publicly available.
- As Mr A progressed, growth became more challenging, requiring him to find ways to surpass competitors.
- In later phases, there was no established precedents to follow, as only a few players had the necessary knowledge and experience. This information was sensitive and not publicly available.
- While Mr A was able to outperform his initial competitors quickly, the competitors he faced in later stages were far more advanced. These competitors had invested year into R&D and had gained substantial experience.

The main lessons from the above two examples are that difficulties tend to increase as we progress in our journey. While growth may come more easily in the initial stages, advancing further often brings tougher competition. In the later phases, the path becomes even more challenging, as only a select few possess the necessary knowledge and experience, and one must often follow precedents set by those who have succeeded before.

The Journey Becomes Harder—Only the Tough Prevail

We can refer to Example 1 and Example 2 discussed earlier to illustrate this point.

In Example 1, Chintan was admitted to the state-level team based on the strong competency and skills he demonstrated in city-level tournaments. However, progressing further was not easy. Once he entered the state team, he now had to compete against the best players from other states. Unlike his previous tournaments, he could no longer score 100+ runs easily in state-level matches.

It is important to note that he was already competent—otherwise, he would not have made it to the state team. But the competition at this level was tougher, and succeeding required further improvement.

In Example 2, Mr A had to continuously find ways to improve in order to drive the next phase of growth. His strong strategic outlook enabled him to expand overseas and surpass many competitors. However, to gain a significant market share from the largest competitor, he later had to develop the best technology at the lowest cost.

They key point here is that if you have come a long way, it means you must have outperformed others. However, the journey will continue to become more challenging, requiring you to grow stronger and better. Perseverance, strategic thinking, and adaptability are essential to overcoming increasingly difficult challenges.

Certain Events May Negatively Impact Your Progress. The One Who Perseveres till the End Reaches the Final Goal

This aspect has been discussed in earlier chapters, so we will cover it briefly here.

Real-Life Example: Enduring and Adaptability in Times of Crisis

The global tourism industry was thriving until January 2020. Suddenly, the COVID-19 pandemic struck, bringing the industry to a standstill. Consider an individual who started a hotel or restaurant just before the pandemic in a location heavily dependent on tourism. Similarly, imagine someone who began investing or trading in stock markets in January 2020, assuming that global markets were performing well.

By March 2020, global markets experienced their sharpest decline since the 2008 financial crisis. At that time, there was no clear outlook on when conditions would improve—whether in months or even years.

Similar situations are unpredictable and may arise multiple times throughout the journey of pursuing a challenging goal. However, those who endured till the end will ultimately succeed. In times of crisis, individual must find alternative solutions to navigate the circumstances.

> *'To extraordinary circumstances, we must apply extraordinary remedies.'*
>
> —Napoleon

17

Struggles Are a Part of the Journey: Embrace Them

This chapter is divided into the following sections:

- Don't get frustrated by your struggles
- Be calm in behaviour, and show aggression in your actions

Don't Get Frustrated by Your Struggles

Real-Life Example: Less Family Support and Exposure to More Struggles

Mr A had two sons: Mr B (the younger son) and Mr C (the elder son). After completing his graduation, Mr C joined his father's business. As Mr C was participating in the family business, he inherited the entirety of his father's wealth. His parents lived with him throughout their lives.

The wealth Mr C inherited was not substantial, but it provided a good starting point. Mr C did not have to struggle for the necessities of life, nor did he need to compromise on basic luxuries. Mr C was not very ambitious and did not want to take risks in life. As he supported his father in the business, he received significant support from his parents throughout life.

In contrast, Mr B was an ambitious person. He quickly realized that joining his father's business, which Mr C was already pursuing, would only divide the pie of available opportunities between the two brothers. Mr B decided to pursue his own dreams and goals.

He chose one of the most challenging paths: attempting the civil services examination. At just eighteen, he had to relocate to a larger town for his studies, leaving behind his friends and living alone in a new environment.

He took up internships with small companies to earn a modest income, becoming self-sufficient and covering his basic needs. Emotionally, he received very limited support from his family. His elder brother, on the other hand, was fortunate to have received both financial and emotional support. Mr B was content with his struggles. He had made his own decisions and chosen a difficult path.

The decision to pursue the civil services exam involved considerable struggles; however, it also presented immense possibilities to achieve something significant. If Mr B succeeded in his journey, all the struggles would be worth it.

Mr B passed the civil services exam through sheer effort, and by the age of fifty, he had reached a top leadership position in the state's revenue department. Had Mr B chosen to join his father's business alongside his brother, his struggles might have been fewer. However, he would have had to share the same wealth, and his opportunities for growth might have been limited.

Even if he had decided to excel in the family's business, his struggles would have been different, but it too would have involved its own challenges.

The summary of this example is simple: if you choose a challenging goal in life, the process will inevitably involve struggles. With great rewards come great responsibilities and struggles. If you have chosen a goal, it is your decision to accept the accompanying struggle. This struggle will, in turn, bring its own rewards.

There is no point comparing your struggles to those of people who have been fortunate enough not to face the same difficulties.

Be Calm in Behaviour, and Show Aggression in Your Actions

At times, the drive to succeed can generate a certain harshness in behaviour. Such harshness may be reflected in your day-to-day activities, including interactions with those around you.

It is important to note that aggression should be confined to the actions that are relevant to achieving your goal. Demonstrating aggression in every aspect of life can be counterproductive. Aggression is necessary to succeed and complete difficult tasks. However, an aspirant needs to understand and train themselves so that aggression is strictly avoided in all other aspects of life. If aggression begins to manifest in your daily behaviour, you may find that there are fewer friends and more enemies around you. The behaviour in your everyday activities should remain calm and composed.

18

Timeframe Matters: Success Takes Time

This chapter is divided into the following sections:

- Understanding the reasonable timeframe required to achieve a goal is crucial
- Strategic planning can shorten the timeframe
- Unexpected challenges can extend the timeframe

Understanding the Reasonable Timeframe Required to Achieve a Goal Is Crucial

In Chapter 7, we discussed that 'small actions over a shorter timeframe generate bigger outcomes over a longer duration—Taj Mahal took twenty-two years to be completed'.

Hence, it is important to have a clear understanding of the broad timeframe required to achieve a challenging goal. Naturally, everyone should aim to achieve goals in as short a duration as possible (that is, it is important to be ambitious). However, if you set an unrealistic timeframe for accomplishing a goal and then compare actual outcomes against it, you may incorrectly conclude that the results are not in line with the desired requirements—even though you may still be on the right path.

A consistent feeling of failure (which may not be actual failure) can lead to frustration and poor decision-making.

Real-Life Example: Setting Realistic Timeframe and Adjusting Strategies Accordingly

Mr A had to travel from location X to location Y, a distance of 1,000 km. He decided to drive his own car instead of taking public transport, believing that this would allow him to reach his destination much faster.

Mr A set a target to reach location Y in just ten hours, aiming for an average speed of 100 km per hour. However, the maximum speed allowed on the highway was 80 km per hour.

For the first 300 km, due to traffic conditions, he could only maintain an average speed of 60 km per hour, taking five hours to cover this distance. The next 200 km took him two and a half hours.

After completing 500 km, he took a short thirty-minute break. During this break, he realized that he had already spent eight hours covering only half the journey. He began to question whether driving his own vehicle was the right decision. Ideally, he should have opted for public transport.

A superfast train typically completes the same journey in twelve hours. Given that he had already spent eight hours covering just 500 km, it was clear that he wouldn't be able to complete the journey within the same timeframe. Moreover, driving for such a long duration—potentially fifteen or more hours—would be extremely exhausting.

We have used similar examples in earlier chapters; however, the key point we want to communicate is that one must be realistic when deciding the broad timeframe.

Additionally, as discussed previously, alongside a long-term goal, it is always beneficial to set short-term goals with indicative timeframes. Observing the outcomes of short-term goals can help answer several critical questions, such as:

- How much time did it take to accomplish the short-term goal?
- Is there a need to adjust the timeframe for the long-term goal?
- Should the approach or direction be changed, or should different resources be utilized to meet the timeframe set for the long-term goal?

Strategic Planning Can Shorten the Timeframe

Continuing the earlier example, after covering approximately 120 km at an average speed of 60 km per hour, Mr A would have quickly realized that completing the entire 1,000 km journey in ten hours was unrealistic.

Upon this realization, he could have explored alternative modes of transportation from his current location. For instance, if there were a nearby public transport hub, he could have parked his car there and switched to public transport to complete the journey. On his return trip to location X, he could have taken public transport back to the same hub and then used his own car to drive home.

Thus, assessing outcomes over a shorter timeframe can help refine strategy, enabling a more efficient approach to achieving the ultimate goal.

Real-Life Example: Strategic Adaptation to Overcome Challenges

A critical army post on a hilltop had been occupied by a group of terrorists. An army battalion of twenty soldiers was assigned the responsibility of reaching the hilltop within the next thirty-six hours and recapturing the post. Any delay in the operation could have allowed the number of terrorists to increase.

The path to the hilltop was extremely challenging. The battalion set out early in the morning at 5.30 a.m., aiming to reach the midway point within ten hours. However, as they climbed, the terrorists kept a close watch on them and engaged in continuous gunfire.

By the time the battalion reached the halfway point, they had lost five team members due to the relentless attack. The terrorists had the advantage of height and a strategic position, allowing them to monitor the battalion's movements and fire easily.

After nine hours of climbing, upon reaching the midway point, the battalion realized that continuing the ascent during daylight might not be a viable strategy. They decided to take a short three-hour break and then climb throughout the night.

The primary objective behind this decision was that, after sunset, the lack of daylight would make the battalion less visible to the terrorists. While climbing at night would be more challenging, it would also make it significantly harder for the terrorists to track their movements. This approach would help prevent further casualties.

Executing their strategy, the battalion climbed for the next twelve hours—throughout the night—and successfully reached the mountain peak early the next morning without losing a single additional team member.

The key takeaway from the above example is the importance of setting a timeline for achieving one's goals. Furthermore, with appropriate strategic planning, these timelines can not only be met but also shortened.

However, it is essential to assess outcomes over shorter intervals in order to refine the strategy, thereby enabling a more efficient approach towards achieving the ultimate goal.

Unexpected Challenges Can Extend the Timeframe

Throughout this book, we have repeatedly acknowledged that certain situations—such as unforeseen mistakes or adverse events—may arise beyond an individual's control and significantly impact their journey.

However, we have also emphasized that such challenges should not deter an aspirant from pursuing their ultimate goal. These situations may lead to delays in achieving a challenging objective, but that should not be a reason to abandon it.

Let us consider a brief example to illustrate the message above:

Real-Life Example: Staying Focused on the Goal Despite an Unexpected Incident

Mr A was preparing for the civil services exams. He cleared the preliminary exam on his first attempt, and his preparation for the mains was going well—he was performing strongly in mock tests.

However, just one week before his mains exam, he met with an accident while driving and had to undergo immediate surgery. He realized that the accident was his mistake, as he had been driving in the wrong direction on the road—a costly error at such a critical time.

The doctor advised complete rest for one month, followed by a six-month recovery period, as the healing process would be slow due to the surgery. This broadly meant that he would be well placed to attempt the exam the following year.

He felt deeply disappointed that, despite all his efforts, he would not get the opportunity to sit for the mains exam. Additionally, he would have to retake the preliminary exam whenever he attempted the exam again.

He decided to attempt the exam in the coming year, although it was still uncertain whether he would be fully prepared. However, postponing his goal by two years could mean losing his chance altogether, as he was only eligible to sit for the civil services exam for the next two years due to the age limit.

After his surgery, Mr A ensured he took good care of his health over the next year while continuing his preparation. In his next attempt, he successfully cleared all three stages—preliminary, mains, and the interview.

Although the timeframe increased by a year, Mr A remained determined and ultimately succeeded in achieving his goal.

Success is often a slow and demanding process, and recognizing the realistic timeframe required is essential to stay committed through setbacks.

19

Your Network Counts: Build a Strong Circle

We have divided this discussion into the following parts:

- Become part of a community or network of like-minded individuals
- You may need support from others when you are stuck—similarly, others may also need your help
- Networking is a habit—some excel at it; others struggle with it. The key lies in finding the right balance
- Even if you are on an independent path, cultivate genuine and meaningful relationships

Become Part of a Community or Network of Like-Minded Individuals

A community or network is a group of individuals pursuing similar goals or engaging in mutually beneficial relationships. For example, such a group may include alumni, competitors, or people offering complementary services or goods. The purpose of a community or association is to provide mutual benefit to its participants.

Therefore, if a relevant community or association exists, an individual aspiring to achieve a challenging goal should engage with it. Participation can offer numerous benefits to the aspirant.

Real-Life Example: Leveraging Networks for Business Growth and Collaboration

Mr A started a textile manufacturing company in Bhilwara (a town in Rajasthan, India). He joined a business association (Group).

His manufacturing business was performing well, and he wanted to expand into wholesale and retail garment trading. Through the Group, he identified a joint venture (JV) partner interested in collaborating for wholesale and retail distribution of the garments produced by his manufacturing facility.

Under the JV arrangement, both Mr A and his partner decided to invest in setting up stores and agreed to share the profits equally. Mr A supplied raw materials at a discounted price, while the JV partner managed and operated the stores.

Both partners faced capital constraints, but through the Group, they connected with a high-net-worth individual (HNI) who was keen to invest in the venture.

Additionally, Mr A gained several other benefits from his association membership—for instance, the Group hosted industry events that helped market the new JV, and he identified multiple retailers interested in purchasing his products.

You May Need Support from Others When You Are Stuck—Similarly, Others May Also Need Your Help

Real-Life Example: The Power of Mutual Support and Networking in Business

Mr Ummed was a property dealer and broker who had recently ventured into real estate development and construction. He identified a large land parcel for construction but needed immediate funds to pay the initial token amount for its purchase.

Seeking assistance, he reached out to multiple members of his business association. One of them, Mr Raman, connected him with a financer who arranged the required funds in a short period, enabling Mr Ummed to secure the land.

Grateful for Mr Raman's support, Mr Ummed developed a strong friendship with him over time. Later, when Mr Raman was setting up a new manufacturing plant, needed help finding a suitable land parcel. Mr Ummed assisted him in securing an excellent deal and also facilitated the entire registration process through his network of local brokers.

The example highlights the importance of seeking help when needed to achieve desired outcomes. However, it is equally important to reciprocate and support others whenever possible, ensuring that relationships remain mutually beneficial in the long run.

Networking Is a Habit—Some Excel at It, Others Struggle with It; the Key Lies in Finding the Right Balance

Many times, it is easy to initiate a new relationship or become part of an association or group. However, maintaining a close connection with the group can be challenging.

This difficulty arises due to our demanding daily routines—we often struggle to find time for ourselves and maintain our health, making it even harder to stay actively involved can become a real challenge.

Therefore, networking is a habit that needs to be developed, and it can have long-term benefits. However, there is no need to set aside other important priorities solely for networking, as such associations may not always yield strong positive outcomes.

The key is to maintain balance—staying connected with the right people so that you can seek support when needed while continuing to grow and move forward in your journey.

Even If You Are on an Independent Path, Cultivate Genuine and Meaningful Relationships

As discussed earlier, even if you join an association or network with others, the competitive environment may make people reluctant to offer help.

Additionally, while many seek support, they often find it difficult to extend the same to others. Over time, providing assistance has also become commercialized, so if a particular form of support benefits your journey, consider obtaining it by paying the necessary price.

When seeking help from competitors, they may be more interested in understanding your challenges rather than offering genuine support. However, not everyone is the same—if you come across sincere individuals, invest in building meaningful relationships.

If you do not find genuine connections, you will have learned the art of walking alone. In such cases, your family members and personal supporters can help fill that gap.

20

Leverage Others: Collaborate for Success

This chapter is divided into the following sections:

- Make it their goal
- Make them feel important and guide them on your journey
- Understand their motivations and reward them appropriately

If you cannot accomplish YOUR goal alone, you must convince and incentivize others to achieve THEIR goals, which is actually aligned with your goal.

The purpose of this book is not to outline traditional team-building or motivation strategies aimed at retaining team members within an organization. Instead, we will focus on how to inspire and engage others in working towards the achievement of our goals.

Make It Their Goal

The first and most crucial step in ensuring that people work towards achieving a challenging goal is to communicate your goal clearly and instil in others the drive to see it as their collective goal, not just yours.

Unless people feel a sense of ownership over the goal, they may participate in the journey but will not take the necessary responsibility. A genuine sense of ownership is essential for success.

Real-Life Example: Building the Right Team by Aligning Individual Aspirations with Business Goals

Mr A started a startup selling electronic gadgets. He aspired to become the No. 1 player in the electronic gadget industry.

To optimize costs and take advantage of cheaper raw materials, the products were manufactured in selected overseas markets. The finished goods were then imported, labelled, marketed, and distributed.

The business required people with the following key skill sets:

- A person or team with a strong network of distributors—responsible for establishing collaborations with distributors to facilitate product sales.
- A person or team to run marketing campaigns—ensuring that advertising spends are utilized effectively and yield the desired outcomes, as reflected in sales figures.
- A person or team with knowledge or experience in product development—responsible for finalizing product designs, identifying manufacturers, negotiating prices, and ensuring compliance with import regulations.
- Support functions—assisting in hiring new team members and securing the necessary finance for setting up and growing the company.

Ideally, a single person may not possess all the required capabilities. Initially, Mr A took on multiple tasks himself to gain a better understanding of the business and acquire the necessary experience.

However, over time, he realized that at least four people were needed to handle these functions independently. He, therefore, had to identify the right individuals who could support him on his journey.

A key challenge was finding these people. Where would he find the right talent? More importantly, many of these individuals were already employed—so why would they leave their jobs to join his startup?

Mr A met various professionals to understand the challenges they faced in their current roles and explored how he could convince them that joining his startup would be beneficial for them.

He identified two individuals who were excelling in their existing roles but desired more autonomy—something they were not getting in their current positions. He realized that granting them greater independence would enable them to perform even better. Mr A successfully hired these two people.

Another two individuals were working in large organizations as part of extensive teams. However, they were keen to take on leadership roles and lead functions independently. They felt they lacked sufficient opportunities to spearhead initiatives despite having a strong preference for leadership and a proactive work style.

Mr A convinced these four individuals that this new organization would not just be another job for them—it would be their organization. Their roles would offer significantly more autonomy, higher responsibility, and the opportunity to earn rewards similar to those of the owners.

With this approach, Mr A built a strong team of individuals who brought diverse skill sets and personal aspirations. He also aligned their aspirations with the business goals.

Furthermore, Mr A fostered a sense of ownership of the broader organizational objectives among his team members, encouraging them to take on the necessary responsibilities.

Make Them Feel Important and Guide Them on Your Journey

The catalyst of a challenging goal, or the person entrusted with the responsibility of achieving it, must take the necessary steps to ensure that team members feel valued in their journey towards success.

People are more motivated when they believe they play a crucial role in accomplishing a goal. While, in theory, everyone may be replaceable, the key lies in making team members feel important and fostering a sense of belonging.

It is essential to remind regularly that their role is critical and that they are the best fit for achieving the goal. If team members lack certain qualities or skills outlined in this book, the catalyst—or the person leading the effort—must support and guide them in developing those capabilities.

Understand Their Motivations and Reward Them Appropriately

People who have joined you on the journey to achieve a goal must be suitably rewarded for their contributions.

To ensure their long-term commitment, they need to receive a fair share on the benefits or outcomes. If they are not adequately rewarded, they may choose to leave or disengage from the journey—even if they are closely aligned with the goal.

Without meaningful rewards, they may feel that they are merely helping to achieve someone else's objective, rather than working towards a goal that also benefits them.

Real-Life Example: Suitably Rewarding Team Members Who Either Want Money or Skin in the Game

Let's continue with the same example used earlier in this chapter—Mr A setting up an electronic gadget venture. Mr A decided not to take a cash salary from the new venture for the next five years. Additionally, he had to make initial investments from his past savings to commence business operations.

There was no immediate certainty of raising funds from third-party investors. Mr A owned the entire equity in the company—meaning that if the company failed, he would lose his savings. However, if he succeeded in his mission, he would be rewarded through the increase in the company's value.

While hiring these four individuals, Mr A offered them a decent salary increment. Additionally, he gave them the option to either take their full salary in cash or become eligible for equity ownership in the company.

Different people chose a mix of cash and equity (including partial equity) for their own reasons.

One individual opted to take up to 70 per cent of his salary in the form of equity instead of cash. This person believed that the company would perform exceptionally well in the future and at the same time, he does not require significant cash. As, he was already investing 70 per cent of his salary in equity stocks of other companies.

After five years, this person requested Mr A to nominate him as a co-founder of the company. He was also willing to invest the necessary capital to acquire up to a 25 per cent stake in the business.

Mr A appreciated the decision, recognizing the individual's long-term vision and commitment to the journey. On the other hand, there was one team member who had opted for 100 per cent cash. After one year of joining the organization, such team member, received a better salary offer elsewhere and moved to another organization.

The primary motivation was a higher salary rather than a deep alignment with the company's mission.

The key takeaway from the above example is that not everyone shares the same motivation drivers or reward expectations.

The aspirant (or catalyst) must closely understand what drives each team member and what they value as a reward. These insights should then be used to effectively align individual motivations with the larger goal, while ensuring team members are rewarded in line with their expectations.

21

Your Real Enemy: The Comfort Zone

This chapter is divided into the following sections:

- You can reach the top—if you have the desire to get there
- If you become satisfied with initial outcomes before achieving your ultimate goal, you are in your comfort zone
- A hunger for better results will push your limits and fuel your desire to reach the top

You Can Reach the Top—If You Have the Desire to Get There

> *'Desire is the starting point of all achievement—not a hope, not a wish, but a keen, pulsating desire that transcends everything.'*
>
> —Napoleon Hill

Many significant records, achievements, and milestones have already been accomplished. Likewise, numerous major inventions and discoveries have taken place. Therefore, one must have a strong desire to take on a challenge in order to set a new record, achieve a milestone, or make an important invention or discovery.

Without the desire to accomplish something unique—something with a low probability of success—we are left only to appreciate past records, achievements, and milestones or to enjoy existing inventions and discoveries.

Having a strong desire to take on a challenge and accomplish it is of utmost importance—it is the starting point.

If there is no desire to achieve something, then this book may not resonate with the reader. In other words, it may not be of interest to someone who lacks the hunger or drive to take on and accomplish a challenge. In such cases, the first step is to cultivate a desire to achieve something challenging.

The majority of people may be content with leading a normal life and may not wish to enter the race to accomplish a difficult goal.

> *'When you vividly imagine the reality of a fulfilled desire and feel the thrill of accomplishment, your subconscious mind works to bring that desire into reality.'*
>
> *—Joseph Murphy*

However, someone with a strong desire to achieve something unique will make every necessary effort and follow the steps outlined in this book to accomplish their goal.

Everyone would be happy to have a credential to their name—whether a record, an achievement, or an accomplishment. After all, success is appealing to everyone.

However, true desire or hunger to accomplish something means being unsatisfied until the goal is achieved. It creates an inner drive to put in relentless effort to reach that goal.

That said, as discussed earlier, having too many desires is counterproductive. If you chase multiple ambitions at once, you may end up achieving none.

For instance, you cannot simultaneously aspire to become the best cricketer and the best entrepreneur. You need to focus on one challenging goal (the method for selecting such a goal is discussed in detail in Chapter 1).

If You Become Satisfied with Initial Outcomes before Achieving Your Ultimate Goal, You Are in Your Comfort Zone

Real-Life Example: Weighing Early Success against Long-Term Ambitions

Amit started a unique skincare product company with the goal of building the largest skincare brand in the country. Through the combined efforts of his entire team and strong strategic decision-making, the company performed exceptionally well in its first five years. It quickly rose to rank among the top five skincare brands in the country.

However, the market leader—the No. 1 skincare brand—was not pleased with the success of this new competitor. To eliminate the competition, the market leader decided to make a lucrative acquisition offer to Amit's company.

The deal was highly attractive for Amit but insignificant for the market leader. Additionally, existing investors pressured Amit to accept the offer and complete the transaction. As financial investors, they had a fixed investment horizon and were primarily interested in securing a high exit multiple. For them, a profitable exit was always the preferred outcome.

Amit was pleased with the offer price and ultimately decided to sell the company. The deal was closed within ten days, and the funds were credited to Amit and the investors' accounts.

Now, with substantial wealth at his disposal, Amit could choose to enjoy life, invest in passive assets, or start a new business. However, his dream of becoming a market leader in the skincare industry could no longer be fulfilled due to the non-compete clause in the exit deal.

There will be many situations where initial outcomes seem favourable. However, if early success leads you into a comfort zone, it can limit your ultimate potential. Amit was satisfied with being ranked among the top five players—a commendable milestone in itself—and chose to abandon his ultimate ambition of becoming a market leader, thus effectively limiting his success in favour of comfort.

A Hunger for Better Results Will Push Your Limits and Fuel Your Desire to Reach the Top

Real-Life Example: The Comfort Zone as a Barrier to Long-Term Growth

Mr X joined an MNC and performed exceptionally well during his first eight years, earning three promotions. He was next in line for a leadership-level promotion. However, the minimum requirement for such a role was twelve years of experience, meaning he would not be eligible for promotion for another four years.

Satisfied with his current designation and role in the organization, he lacked a strong desire to reach the top leadership level. The role was challenging, involved significant responsibilities, and required an equity contribution to the organization, which he was reluctant to take on.

Over the next five years, his peers were promoted to leadership positions, while he remained in the same role. However, he never reached that level because he did not push himself in the direction required to attain a leadership role.

Over time, he also stopped feeling disappointed that his peers had moved ahead of him, even though he had been ahead of them in the past. Instead, he became comfortable with his existing position—a comfort zone that ultimately became the real enemy of his future growth, despite all the potential he possessed.

The key takeaway here is that to achieve long-term objectives, the level of desire and commitment (as discussed in this book) must remain consistent over the years.

You must continue to push your limits and strive for better results. While it is important to celebrate achievement, there should always be a hunger to accomplish even more.

Benchmarks should keep rising, and one must make continuous efforts to meet and exceed them. If your benchmark is too low, and achieving it gives you a sense of complete satisfaction, then there will be no further scope for improvement.

Such outcomes may not be sufficient to compete with stronger candidates—those who relentlessly push their limits to keep improving over time.

22

Survival Mode: Find a Way to Stay Afloat

This discussion has been divided into the following parts:

- Your competitors will be happy when you are struggling—why would they help you?
- Your well-wishers may offer emotional support, but they cannot fight your battles for you
- You must leverage your strengths and find ways to stay afloat
- Once you overcome a difficult situation, analyse the reasons for your struggles and work on those weakness.

Your Competitors Will Be Happy When You Are Struggling—Why Would They Help You?

In the journey of accomplishing a challenging goal, there will be many situations where you need guidance or direction from someone who can offer support based on their own experience (mentorship).

However, not everyone has access to the right mentor. Even if you do not have one, they may not always have the time to support you on every occasion. Additionally, a mentor must be genuinely willing to provide the necessary guidance or direction, regardless of their own benefit.

In difficult situations, people often end up discussing their problems with others who speak politely and show empathy, without fully knowing whether those individuals are well-wishers—or even competitors.

Everyone participates in a challenge to win. At times, people may take advantage of your difficult situations for their own benefit and may even misguide you into making incorrect decisions.

When facing difficulties, stay strong and avoid discussing your problems with everyone around you. Remember, you are walking your own path—whether or not you share your problems with others, you must ultimately find your own solutions. Do not expect others to help.

Your Well-Wishers May Offer Emotional Support, But They Cannot Fight Your battles for You

If you are struggling to find a solution to a particular problem on your journey, your well-wishers may offer emotional support. However, it may be unrealistic to expect them to resolve the problem for you.

They may not have the necessary experience to handle the various challenges that arise when working towards a challenging goal.

In certain situations, your elders or seniors may be able to connect you with others who have faced similar challenges and might be able to help.

Real-Life Example: The Risk of Stagnation

Vinay was a first-generation entrepreneur in his family. His parents were government employees—his father was a bank manager at a nationalized government bank, and his mother was a university lecturer.

Vinay was pursuing a unique, technology-driven business idea. However, he was a chartered account with a background in accounting, tax, and finance.

His friends worked in large MNCs, including private equity funds. They could have helped him set up meetings for an elevator pitch and supported him in fundraising.

However, the key challenge was finding someone to develop the technology platform—at least a prototype.

Without someone with a strong technology background who also has a stake in the new venture, why would investors support it?

The key challenge, therefore, was to find someone who could develop the technology platform and continue to maintain, improve, and scale it over time.

Vinay discussed this challenge with his parents and close friends. A few suggestions emerged:

- Hiring a third-party vendor to develop the prototype by paying a fee
- Finding a co-founder with a technology background
- Hiring a senior-level CTO

However, these were common solutions that Vinay was already aware of.

His parents and close family members tried to support him as much as they could, but they were unable to bridge this critical gap.

No family member or friend knew someone willing to quit their existing job and join the startup. Nor had they come across a third party that could develop the technology platform and take equity in the company in exchange for building and maintaining it.

However, investors would prefer someone who could run the business full-time, possessed the necessary skill set (a strong academic background with relevant experience), and was willing to take the required risk—accepting a nominal salary while holding a majority equity stake. His friends and family were unable to help him further in solving this challenge.

Ultimately, Vinay found a co-founder through a social media platform and successfully raised equity funding from investors to build the business.

You Must Leverage Your Strengths and Find Ways to Stay Afloat

Real-Life Example: Adapting to Workplace Demands with Efficiency and Strategy

Harpreet joined an MNC one and a half years ago. During his time there, he had very long office hours, averaging ten hours a day. His job also required him to work on certain weekends. Initially, he found it difficult to adjust. While he was comfortable working long hours on weekdays, working on weekends was challenging, as he needed that time to recharge.

He discussed this challenge with close family members. They suggested that if the workload was too demanding and he could not adapt to this work culture in the long term, he should consider leaving and exploring other options.

Harpreet also came across different peers who had various ways of dealing with the challenge:

- Some were not as efficient as Harpreet but were comfortable working on weekends.
- Some were neither as efficient as Harpreet nor willing to work on weekends. As a result, they received lower appraisal ratings due to poor performance. They accepted slightly lower rankings and frequently faced negative feedback for missing target timelines.
- Some were neither as efficient as Harpreet nor willing to work on weekends. These individuals chose to quit the company and continued switching jobs for years. Despite their struggles, they were unable to find a sustainable solution to their challenge.

Over time, Harpreet realized that such a work culture had become standard across the industry. He focused on building the skills needed to perform his tasks more efficiently. By optimizing his productivity during the five weekday workdays, he ensured that he was not required to work on weekends—except in unavoidable situations. Harpreet found his own way to stay afloat.

Once You Overcome a Difficult Situation, Analyse the Reasons for Your Struggle and Work on Those Weaknesses

Real-Life Example: Balancing Strengths and Weaknesses for Long-Term Success

Hardik was a member of the national cricket team and played as an all-rounder. He handled fast bowlers well, but his batting performance was inconsistent. Moreover, he struggled on pitches that favoured spin bowlers.

A new batting coach had recently joined the team. While reviewing Hardik's performance, he realized that spin bowlers could dismiss him easily. He told Hardik that the main reason for his inconsistent performance was his weakness against spin bowlers.

A crucial match was scheduled in two days, but this short timeframe was not enough for Hardik to develop strong batting skills against spinners. However, in two days, he learned to handle spin bowlers—meaning he would not get out easily, though he might not score well.

During the critical match, while he merely managed the spinners' overs, his performance against fast bowlers was excellent. As a result, his overall batting performance in the match was very good. However, he realized that this strategy would not be effective in the long run. Over the next six months, he worked on facing spin bowlers to improve his overall batting record.

The purpose of this example is to highlight that when an aspirant is aware of their shortcomings, they should take all necessary steps to address them. However, in some situations, weaknesses cannot be corrected immediately and require sustained effort over a longer period to yield favourable results. In such cases, the aspirant should maximize their strengths to achieve the best possible outcomes while gradually working on their weaknesses.

23

Be Politically Savvy: Choose Wisely

This chapter is divided into the following sections:

- Clashing with power can end your journey
- Staying neutral is risky—if you neither oppose nor support power, you may still be sidelined, as power favours its own
- Aligning with power may provide support and opportunities for growth
- Power is not permanent—it constantly changes

Clashing with Power Can End Your Journey

Real-Life Example: The Importance of Political Awareness in Business and Leadership

Mr G started a business with a strong government focus, specifically in power generation through renewable energy sources.

The government aimed to have large local business players generate power and supply it to the government-owned power grid. Mr G was awarded a large contract to supply power to the grid. However, after three years, a serious conflict arose between Mr G and a powerful government official.

The contract was due for renewal but was unfortunately not extended. Instead, it was awarded to another industrialist with closer ties to government officials.

After losing this contract, no other government-owned power grid awarded contracts to Mr G due to resistance from top-level officials.

With restrictions on supplying power, distribution to private players was also not permitted. As a result, over time, Mr G was forced to shut down the business.

The key takeaway here is that as you progress in your journey, there will be situations where being politically astute is essential for survival and growth.

Regardless of the circumstances, there is no room for conflict or confrontation with those in power. If a clash with power arises, every effort should be made to resolve it politely. Otherwise, the journey may become extremely difficult or come to an abrupt end.

This issue is particularly prevalent in large organizations and businesses, where there is always someone in a higher position with greater authority and influence.

Staying Neutral Is Risky—If You Neither Oppose Nor Support Power, You May Still Be Sidelined, as Power Favours Its Own

This refers to a situation where a person chooses to remain politically neutral, avoiding involvement in political issues or power dynamics.

Real-Life Example: The Limitations of Neutrality in Power-Driven Environments

Continuing from the previous example, it is important to note that Mr G would never have been awarded the initial contract to start his business if he had not built the necessary connections with those responsible for awarding contracts. Insiders play a crucial role in such decisions.

Therefore, even if Mr G were to resolve his conflict with those in power, he would not automatically regain his previous standing or become a preferred choice for future contracts.

At best, he would move from being on the adverse side to a neutral position. However, even in this situation, he would struggle—despite his efforts, he would not receive the necessary support or opportunities.

The problem in such situations is that no matter how much effort you put into succeeding in your journey, if you remain neutral or try to maintain good relations with multiple sides, others will eventually take advantage of you without offering any rewards in return.

Over time, you will come to realize that staying neutral does not help in achieving the desired benefits or outcomes.

Aligning with Power May Provide Support and Opportunities for Growth

Real-Life Example: Maintaining Strategic Relationships for Long-Term Stability

Continuing from the earlier example, if Mr G had avoided conflict with those in power, he would have continued to receive their support for years to come. It was Mr G's responsibility to ensure that no conflict arose with those in power. Even if disagreements occurred, leading to temporary setbacks, they should have been resolved tactfully and with patience.

The key takeaway here is that an aspirant must maintain good relations with those in power. Any situation that leads to disagreement should be handled politely and resolved carefully.

Remember, as long as there in an opportunity to stay aligned with power and received the necessary support and growth, there is no benefit in alienating those in control.

Power Is Not Permanent—It Constantly Changes

One of the most difficult challenges arises when you are closely aligned with those in power, but a shift occurs at the top level.

In such situations, re-aligning with the new power can be particularly challenging. The new leadership will have its own preferences, favouring long-time supporters.

Additionally, your loyalty may be questioned, requiring you to prove your allegiance before successfully re-aligning yourself.

Real-Life Example: The Risks of Power Dependence and Leadership Transitions

Continuing with the example of Mr G discussed earlier, let's assume there was no conflict between him with any government official.

As a result, things were going smoothly for Mr G. He was reaping the benefits of his connections with those in power. His contracts were easily renewed, and he was consistently awarded new ones. However, a shift in power occurred—whether due to the retirement of officials or an election. With the new leadership in place, Mr G was no longer a preferred choice, as he had been closely associated with the previous officials. The new officials wanted to bring in their own people and award them the contracts. As a result, Mr G was no longer in a favourable position.

The new officials began identifying deficiencies in his pricing, performance, and other key parameters. They started portraying Mr G as someone who was not serving the larger interests of the nation, placing him under intense scrutiny. Suddenly, inquiries were launched against Mr G and his company. It is important to note that in power-driven environments, being politically unaware or neutral can quietly end a journey that has barely begun. Success often hinges not just on merit, but on the wisdom to align strategically and adapt as power shifts.

24

Loyalty and Trust: Foundations of Success

We have divided this chapter into the following sections:

- Trust in your capabilities
- Faith in God
- Loyalty towards your supporters and well-wishers

Trust in Your Capabilities

As discussed in previous chapters, an aspirant must cultivate self-belief and optimism.

Many times, during the journey, self-doubt may arise—questions like 'Will I ever succeed, or will all my efforts go to waste?' may surface.

However, if others can accomplish their goals, so can you. Keep putting in the effort, and over time, you will develop the necessary capabilities to succeed—because there is no alternative to achieving your goal.

Always remember that success is not a choice but a necessity.

Faith in God

In a highly competitive environment, as discussed earlier, you may often find yourself walking alone on the road to success. If you wish to achieve your goal, you must do it on your own.

Such competition can sometimes lead to feelings of loneliness, making it essential to have faith in something greater than yourself.

This faith can provide inner strength—the belief that there is someone who will support you when you need it most, whether it be fate, destiny, or divine intervention.

While hard work and effort are crucial, luck also plays a role in success. Have faith in the Almighty or in anyone or anything you deeply believe in.

Loyalty towards Your Supporters and Well-Wishers

Throughout your journey, there will be people who stand by you and offer their support. When they need your help, take that opportunity to give back.

As discussed earlier, it is essential to support others when they seek your assistance—loyalty and gratitude strengthen relationships and pave the way for long-term success.

25

Adapt Your Goals: Pivot When Necessary

We have divided this chapter into the following sections:

- When a better opportunity arises, and you have the ability to take on more risk
- When rewards are not commensurate with the risks assumed, and there is no ability to manage future risks

There are many situations where individuals, despite taking all the right steps, feel they are not on the correct path. In such cases, it is crucial to assess whether a change in approach—or even in the ultimate goal itself—is necessary.

This chapter will explore key scenarios where revisiting and adjusting your goals become essential.

When a Better Opportunity Arises, and You Have the Ability to Take on More Risk

Real-Life Example: Taking Calculated Risks to Pursue Greater Aspirations

Let's take the example of Mr D. Mr D completed his education at a top engineering college. He then pursued management education at a globally accredited premier institute.

Mr D's father was very wealthy. However, he took an education loan to fund his entire studies (engineering and management education).

The key reasons behind this loan obligation were:

- The education loan was comparatively cheaper, and his father could generate better returns from the same capital.
- He wanted Mr D to fund his own education so that he would take his studies seriously, knowing that he had a liability to repay upon completing his education.

Mr D secured one of the most coveted jobs through his college placement. The annual package was a dream figure for many candidates in his batch.

Mr D was also happy and joined the job. He performed well in his job for five years. His performance ratings were excellent, and he received good bonuses and promotions. During these five years, he was able to repay the entire loan. However, he was unable to accumulate substantial savings.

Given that his father was very wealthy, he realized that his potential for wealth generation in a job would be limited unless he attained a leadership role in the future. His ultimate goal was to create significant wealth, which he believed could only be achieved by becoming a business owner.

Mr D was comfortable with having no savings for the next five years. Over the past five years, he had realized that the money he could have saved would not have made a substantial difference—an amount his father could easily afford.

Mr D decided to start a business and create wealth for himself over the long term. He consulted his father, who told him that he would not be able to support him financially in this new business venture. His father emphasized that this was a decision Mr D needed to make independently.

Around this time, he married his college batchmate.

Mr D quit his high-paying job, a decision that many believed was unwise. To them, it seemed like a far-fetched dream to build a successful business and generate substantial wealth.

His wife continued working for the next five years, and they managed their living expenses through her salary. Over the next ten years, Mr D built a company that ranked among the top 100.

The key takeaway here is to believe in better opportunities that align with your aspirations and not be afraid to seize them.

However, be mindful that the outcomes of choosing a different path may be worse than those you might have achieved by staying on your original course.

That said, remember that risk and reward are correlated, as discussed earlier in Chapter 2.

When Rewards Are Not Commensurate with the Risks Assumed, and There Is No Ability to Manage Future Risks

Real-Life Example: Recognizing Unmanageable Risks

Let's continue with the example of Mr D and assume an adverse situation. While working, Mr D started trading stocks and index derivatives. Over his five-year job period, he made money through trading.

During this time, he acquired all the necessary skills, such as technical analysis, position sizing, and risk management. Hence, he quit his job, believing he could become a full-time trader in stocks and index derivatives.

Over the next year, he suffered a small loss. However, he did not give up and continued refining his trading strategies.

Over the following two years, he continued to incur losses and eventually realized that stock and index derivative trading was feasible only through algorithm-based machines.

He had neither the vision nor the expertise to undertake trading through algorithm-based systems. Though the idea was promising, he failed to manage the risks effectively.

After three years, he returned to a job, having understood that derivative trading is pure speculation unless handled professionally with the necessary infrastructure.

Thus, taking risks is not a problem. However, if you realize that the risk outweighs the rewards and you have no means to manage them, there is no point in continuing to take unwarranted risks.

26

Own Your Success: It's Your Responsibility

We have kept this chapter very short to cover an obvious yet crucial discussion: your success is your responsibility. You cannot expect others to make you succeed.

We have already discussed this issue at multiple points in this book. However, let's consider one example.

Real-Life Example: Taking Ownership of Your Goals and Efforts

Master Aditya was an average student during his school days, consistently scoring average grades in academics. His participation in co-curricular activities was minimal.

During parent-teacher meetings, his parents would blame the school faculty for his poor performance. They argued that, as both of them were working professionals, they had very little time to devote to Aditya's learning and development. Since Aditya spent most of his time at school, they believed that his teachers had the primary responsibility for his academic progress.

At these meetings, the parents would also emphasize that they were working hard in their own jobs to afford

Aditya's school fees. Beyond paying the fees, they felt there was little they could do to improve his performance.

As a result, Aditya developed a mindset from an early age: if you are paying for a support or service, you have the right to expect guaranteed results.

After completing his schooling, Aditya's parents enrolled him in coaching for the civil services exam. However, his performance was very poor in his initial attempt.

In contrast, one of his friends, Chintan, cleared all the levels on his first attempt. Chintan came from a poor family, with only his father as the earning member. His parents could not afford the necessary resources for civil services exam preparations.

Despite this, his parents told him, 'There is very little we can do to help.' However, Chintan realized that he needed to put in the effort to succeed and build a better future for himself.

Aditya was unhappy with his results and asked Chintan what he should do to succeed in his next attempt. Chintan advised him, 'Stop expecting help from everyone—your parents, teachers, or friends. If you truly want to crack the civil services exam, remember that it is your goal and your dream.'

He explained further, 'Teachers can help improve your performance, but they cannot be blamed for poor results. There are thousands of students who seek their guidance, and that is why they enrol in coaching. Even if many students fail and blame their teachers, those teachers will continue to earn their livelihood. Every year, new talented students join their classes, and as long as some of them succeed, the teachers will always have success stories to showcase.'

The simple yet crucial message of the above example is this: Your success is your responsibility—you cannot expect others to make you succeed.

Given the same set of resources, some individuals will go on to achieve their goals, while others may fail dramatically. Taking full responsibility for one's goals is a fundamental requirement.

If the aspirant relies on others for success, the likelihood of achieving the desired outcome is very slim.

In most cases, the key difference between success and failure is not a lack of resources—many people succeed despite limited means, as demonstrated by several examples in this book—but rather a weak foundation, marked by a lack of ownership and personal responsibility for the goal.

27

Yeh Dil Maange More: Set Your Next Goal

This is the final chapter of this book.

If you have successfully accomplished a challenging goal, it is now time to repeat the steps you have already implemented.

Once a challenging goal has been achieved, you should set your sights on the next one. This is how we continue to grow and make history.

Real-Life Example: Building a Global Quick Commerce Giant

Mr A started a quick commerce company with the ambition of building one of the largest such companies in the country. Over the next twenty years, he adopted best practices—including many outlined in this book—and successfully built one of the biggest quick commerce businesses in India. His initial goal had been achieved.

Although, Mr A was satisfied with this success, he aspired to take the company much further. He decided to expand operations internationally. He commissioned market research across a few selected countries and, based on the findings, identified significant potential in the Middle East, Asia, and North America.

After becoming a leading player in India, he decided to take on a global challenge. His dream was to list the company on international stock exchanges.

After deciding to go global, he adopted a mixed business strategy, which included both organic growth and inorganic growth (that is, acquiring companies that offered delivery services and had existing fleet and staff).

He developed local business development and strategic teams in each identified market. The responsibility of these teams was to execute the expansion and operational plans.

The global expansion plan was successful, and over the next thirty years, the company became one of the largest quick commerce companies in the world.

Once again, the time had come to take on a new challenge.

Mr A now dreamed of making his company the largest global consumer services company. The horizon was not limited to grocery delivery; he aimed to cover all possible avenues of e-commerce, including end-to-end retail trading of electronics, apparels, and more. His goal was to explore all 360-degree possibilities.

To accomplish this, he faced intense competition from large global players. However, certain synergies already existed (such as the delivery fleet, warehouses, and staff) that could be leveraged for the new expansion.

The key to Mr A's success in reaching the top was his ability to consistently accomplish his goals and take on new, challenging ones.

The key takeaway is that in the journey to the top, it is critical to accomplish challenging goals. However, it is equally important to continually identify the next phase of growth and challenges.

Only a few people will reach the top. If an aspirant desires to become an undefeated leader, it is essential to always think about the next phase of growth and the challenges ahead. The goalposts will continue to evolve over time.

About the Authors

Anuj Jain is a chartered accountant and company secretary by qualification, holding a BCom degree from University of Rajasthan's Commerce College. Born and brought up in Jaipur, Anuj cleared both CA and CS in his first attempts. With over a decade of professional experience, he currently serves as a director in Deloitte India's M&A team, where he advises on complex mergers, acquisitions, restructurings, and strategic initiatives including IPOs and fundraisers. Anuj began his career with EY before joining Deloitte, and has played a pivotal role in some of India's most significant M&A transactions.

Apart from his corporate role, Anuj is a passionate entrepreneur and investor. He ventured into derivative trading in 2019 and has grown steadily through continuous learning, experience, and resilience. Known for his ambition, self-motivation, and results-driven approach, Anuj continues to balance his professional career and entrepreneurial pursuits.

Anshika Jain is an entrepreneur and homemaker with a strong academic foundation in commerce. Born and raised in Kishangarh, Rajasthan, she completed her MCom from MDS University, Ajmer, and cleared the intermediate level of the company secretary course. In 2018, she moved to Gurugram, Haryana, with her husband, Anuj Jain.

Anshika is deeply committed to both her entrepreneurial ventures and family life, balancing the two with grace and dedication. She believes in the power of teamwork and brings this value into every aspect of her personal and professional journey. Her grounded upbringing and strong educational background continue to shape her approach to life and work.